GW01458170

Maralinga Man:

Tales of the Squadron Leader

Sir Arthur Lawrence

Text copyright © Sir Arthur Lawrence 2017
Design copyright © Rowanvale Books 2017
All rights reserved.

Sir Arthur Lawrence has asserted his right under the Copyright, Designs and Patents Act 1988 to be identified as the author of this work.

This book is meant to be educational, informative and entertaining. The anecdotes are recounted as accurately as possible from the author's perspective, with a little embellishment for the reader's entertainment, and are reflections of real conversations and events that took place. Although the author and publisher have made every effort to ensure that the information in this book was correct at the time of publication, the author and publisher do not assume and hereby disclaim any liability to any party for loss, damage or disruption caused by errors or omissions, whether such errors or omissions result from negligence, accident or any other cause.

No part of this book may be reprinted or reproduced or utilised in any form or by electronic, mechanical or any other means, now known or hereafter invented, including photocopying or recording, or in any information storage or retrieval system, without the permission in writing from the Publisher and Author.

First published 2017
by Rowanvale Books Ltd
The Gate
Keppoch Street
Roath
Cardiff
CF24 3JW
www.rowanvalebooks.com

A CIP catalogue record for this book is available from the British Library.
ISBN: 978-1-911240-78-5

DEDICATED TO

ALL THOSE WHO SERVED

AT

MARALINGA RANGE

AND

CHRISTMAS ISLAND

ACKNOWLEDGEMENTS

Alison Butters. For typing and editing.

Gerda Semple. My neighbour. For suggestions.

John Desmond Searle RN (Ret'd). My longest serving friend. For further suggestions.

Jay Rixon. Designer at Rowanvale Books. For Illustrations.

Contents

EXPLANATORY NOTE

60 years ago I found myself serving the Royal Air Force on a rocket testing site in the South Australian desert, 700 miles from the nearest town. By way of some slight relief from boredom, I began to keep a loose-leaf diary of anecdotes and conversations, with the central character being my Commanding Officer. The Squadron Leader was a man of extraordinary appearance and powerful charisma. Although a martinet, he also had a very good sense of humour.

After the Squadron Leader and I had retired from the RAF, we came together again quite by chance. I continued to make notes of his very unusual lifestyle, adding them to my diaries, which had travelled with me since the 1960s.

My notes lay gathering dust in my office until a recent, determined spring clean by my lady wife unearthed them. This book is an accurate revival of conversations and events. There has been some exaggeration and embellishment for the entertainment of the reader. Names have been changed to protect the guilty.

Introduction

So you want to meet the Squadron Leader? You must want to, otherwise you would not have bought, borrowed or stolen this book.

Well, the Squadron Leader doesn't want to meet you. The Squadron Leader does not wish to meet anyone. The Squadron Leader considers that 98% of the human race is suffering from idiocy and he believes himself in grave danger of being infected.

No matter. I shall tell you all I know of the Squadron Leader and through that you will effectively have met him. But first it is necessary for you to understand how I came to meet the Squadron Leader. Later you will come to realise why I detested him and yet became a life-long friend, happy to assist him in any situation.

Aged 18 I was called up for National Service. I opted to sign on as a short-term Regular, in the hope of obtaining a commission. Eventually I was sent on an officers' training course at RAF Uxbridge. In the final stages of this course I faced an interview board. The result of this was that my commission was deferred and I was to apply again in six months.

I was then transferred to an adjoining camp at RAF Hillingdon. This had originally been an old Manor House, surrounded by wooded land. This camp also housed a substantial contingent of WRAF personnel. Due to the woods allowing direct access onto the camp, the unit was considered vulnerable to nighttime intruders. Accordingly, there was a daily roster of all night patrols. This was voluntary, unless the required numbers were not forthcoming. Anyone performing the duty was given the next

24 hours off duty. I frequently put my name on the list for it suited me to clear off to my home in nearby North London when duty was finished.

I had been at Hillingdon about five months when I was called to the office of the Station Adjutant. I was told that on six occasions within the past three months, different Women's Royal Air Force personnel had been disciplined upon being caught emerging from the out-of-bounds woods in the early morning hours in various states of undress. I was further informed that I had been on night duty on every occasion. I pointed out that I had been on night duty many other times when presumably no such incidents had occurred. I was told this was irrelevant and that, in any event, I was to be posted overseas. "As far away as possible" were the Adjutant's exact words. My protests that I was due for a review of my application for a commission were laughed at.

The posting turned out to be Maralinga Range, in the South Australian desert, where the Blue Streak nuclear missile was being tested.

The saga of my transportation from RAF Lynham to Maralinga Range by converted Lancaster bomber would make a series of short stories in themselves. They are not the subject of this book. Suffice it to say that a journey which ought to have taken four days took seven weeks and encompassed glorious breaks in Ceylon (now Sri Lanka) and Singapore. Finally, in 1960, I arrived in Maralinga, ready to report to the RAF Unit and to meet for the first time Squadron Leader Folly.

ONE
We Meet The Squadron Leader

The Lancaster dumped me in Darwin, amongst a million mosquitoes. After a sleepless night under the nets I was transferred to Maralinga in a plane so small that I feared for my life. As we swooped down towards Maralinga Range, all I could see for miles around was bushland and desert. Suddenly a settlement appears; it is an Aboriginal reservation, much like those the Red Indians were confined to in the Wild West days of America. Yet this was the modern Australia of the 1960s. As I write this, 50 years onwards, the situation has changed very little.

On landing at the desolate missile testing range, I was told to report to the Regimental Sergeant Major's office immediately. Arriving there, I found a somewhat perplexed Australian Army RSM.

"You are Senior Aircraftsman Gooner, are you not?"

"Yes, Regimental Sergeant Major."

"The British Royal Air Force were expecting a Flt Lt Gooner, are there two of you?"

"No, Sir. I was due for commission review board when I was suddenly posted here."

"Well you've taken a damned long time getting here. You had better explain yourself to Squadron Leader Folly, and good luck to you."

This sounded a bit ominous and I was soon to find out why. The RSM took me to the Squadron Leader's office and announced me formally as SAC Gooner. The Squadron Leader is about four feet ten inches and weighs around 30 stone. He has a large, concave indentation on the left side of his head, courtesy of his service as a Rear Gunner on Lancasters during the Second World War. His eyes bulged beyond the plane of his face. He was not a pretty sight.

I present my papers.

"What the hell is this? I made an indent for an Accounting Officer six weeks ago. All I've had since are these." He throws down a sheaf of several telexes. "Finally they send me an SAC and where the hell have you been?"

I explained the circumstances.

"Not your fault. Another Air Ministry foul up for me to sort out. Report to Sgt Wilson in EPAS for the time being."

Sgt Wilson turned out to be a pipe cleaner thin individual, say five foot nine inches in height and probably seven stone in weight. He is timid and stutters and, though only in his thirties, he has the pallor of an old man; subsequently I conclude that this is the result of a year's service under the Squadron Leader's command. His aspect is not improved when he walks, since his feet splay out in a 20 minutes to four position. Another who is not a pretty sight.

Sgt Wilson takes me back to a very small office, immediately next to the Squadron Leader's office. Here he hands me a large journal and two trays, piled high with RAF forms.

"This is a copy of the Range Inventory of Equipment and the unposted requisitions for withdrawal and return of items. I did start to make entries myself but the Squadron Leader turned nasty and said I was incompetent. I suggest you study everything but do nothing until the Squadron Leader decides what to do about your posting." With that he shuffled off.

Two days drift by. On the morning of the third day, there is a loud thump on the plasterboard wall of my cubby hole and a deep baritone voice roars, "Mr Gooner." I scuttle around and present myself in the Squadron Leader's office.

"An Officers' Review Board will be held on Thursday at Headquarters Far Eastern Command, RAF Edinburgh Fields, Adelaide. You will attend. Sgt Wilson will arrange a seat on our supply plane on Wednesday. Check with him about accommodation. You will report to me at 2pm on Friday with details of your commission. If your commission is not confirmed, tell Sgt Wilson but do not come near me. Dismissed."

I duly attend the Officers' Board at Edinburgh Fields. It is obvious to me that the Squadron Leader has made his feelings known. I am given a cursory examination and am granted my commission. I return to the Squadron Leader with the good news.

"What rank have you passed out with?"

"Pilot Officer, Sir."

"Damn them. I have a requirement for a Flight Lieutenant. By my authority, and with immediate effect, you are appointed Acting Flight Lieutenant, unpaid. Now get started on that Inventory and let me have the total figures for each unit hub-a-dub[1]. I want the General off my back."

[1.] Old Far Eastern command slang meaning very quickly

7

A bemused Gooner is advised by the Squadron Leader of his requirements.

The Squadron Leader is referring to General Charles, the Range Commander. The mention of each unit refers to the make-up of the Combined Services Task Force at Maralinga: these comprised individual units from the British Army, Navy and Royal Air Force, the same from the Australian services, a Canadian unit and a unit from New Zealand. It is appropriate to mention here that service at Maralinga Range was nominated Active Duty, which gave the Squadron Leader rather more authority and licence than he normally would have had; and you may be sure that he took full advantage of the situation.

Maralinga was an all male unit, numbering about 400 personnel. It was 700 miles from the nearest town (Adelaide) and 700 miles from the nearest woman. None of this bothered the Squadron Leader. He had a constant friend who brought him great comfort at all times. The friend's name was Johnnie Walker (Black Label).

TWO
The Squadron Leader Takes To The Bottle

The Squadron Leader's one and only friend was whisky. Not any whisky, but Johnnie Walker Black Label; he would never drink anything else. On one occasion in the Mess, the Steward, having no Black Label left in stock, served the Squadron Leader with Johnnie Walker Red Label. The Squadron Leader took one sip then hurled the glass, complete with the whisky, back over the bar.

"Never serve me with this filth again," he roared.

The Catering Officer came over and asked if anything was wrong. The Squadron Leader gave him a look so withering it would have paralysed a snake. He said: "This dumbhead knows what I drink, but has attempted to serve me an inferior brand whilst no doubt charging my account with Johnnie Black. See that he is put on a charge."

"Sir," said the distraught Bar Steward, "I am sorry but we have run out of Black Label."

The Squadron Leader glared at the Catering Officer. "This incompetent," he said, "has done no proper stocktaking or ordering. See that he is put on a charge." With this the Squadron Leader stormed out of the Mess. He returned a few minutes later, his face glowing with good cheer.

"Everything alright, Sir?" I asked.

"It is now. That new batman you found me is on the ball. He laid in fresh supplies in my donga[2] this morning. But really the services on this Range have reached a new low when one has to serve oneself from one's own provisions. Let's go and get some fuel inside us."

With that the Squadron Leader took his seat at table and proceeded to demolish a five-course meal. He even condescended to pass a little inconsequential conversation with others at the table. This was most unusual.

I had been ensconced in my cubby hole next to the Squadron Leader's office only a few days before I realised that every day, promptly at 2pm, a Bar Steward delivered a brown paper bag to the Squadron Leader's office. I suspected this was a bottle of Johnnie Walker Black Label, but what I did not suspect was that the Squadron Leader would imbibe the whole bottle before leaving the office at the invariable time of 4pm. All became clear several days later when I first became aware of what was to prove a continuous pattern of actions. At 4pm the sound of glass smashing came from the Squadron Leader's office, followed immediately by the heavy thump of his 30 plus stones departing along the bare, wooden corridor of Headquarters. As soon as the sound subsided, I went into the Squadron Leader's office. There I found the broken remains of a Johnnie Walker bottle, empty, of course. Having drained the tipple which gave him so much pleasure and finding the bottle empty, he simply threw it against the wall. This sequence continued throughout the 18 months which I served on the Range.

[2] Hut

THREE
Batman Trouble

One of the early jobs the Squadron Leader lumbered me with was to find him a batman to replace his existing man, who had requested a return to general duties. The matter ought to have been dealt with by Sgt Wilson, but, as the Squadron Leader was frequently to tell me, "the man is incompetent". In fairness to Wilson, he had on three occasions, prior to my arrival, provided the Squadron Leader with a new batman. The problem was the Squadron Leader's behaviour. He insisted on his daily requirements being carried out exactly. He must be woken exactly on time, accompanied by a tumbler of Johnnie Walker Black Label. His shower must be turned on five minutes later. Clean clothing and freshly pressed uniform must be laid out. Bed linen was to be changed daily. These latter demands would have been more easily carried out if it were not for the Squadron Leader's occasional incontinence and diarrhoea. His foul temper was notorious.

Sgt Wilson maintained he had no one else available. When I told him that "no" was not an option, he produced the names of two general duties men, SAC William Smithson and AC2 "Jock" Mulcahy. "My advice, Sir," said Wilson, "would be to try persuasion. Ordering them will only lead to disaster." Smithson I immediately dismissed from my mind, knowing him to be an undisciplined "Jack the Lad". Mulcahy I did not know. I reviewed his record. On the Range for three months; mainly cleaning and cookhouse duties; already been charged on four occasions for minor offences, e.g. no cap, late for work, drinking alcohol outside of permitted areas.

I interviewed Mulcahy and came straight to the point:

"Jock, will you take the job?"

"Well, I'll take the job, Sir, and I'll give satisfaction, but only on one condition."

"No conditions, Jock, but I can hear a request."

"Then my request, Sir, is that if I am put on any petty charge, then it will be heard by yourself. I cannot come up on another charge before the Squadron Leader."

"I cannot hear charges, Jock. The best I can do is to try to get them dropped if they are not serious."

"I rely upon you, Sir."

"Very well, Jock, you will start on Monday morning. In the meantime, make sure you get the fullest details of the Squadron Leader's requirements from his batman."

I did not realise the problems dealing with Jock's charges would give me. I had to engage in a plethora of pleas, excuses and refusals to several ranks, from a Naval Warrant Officer up to the Camp Adjutant, an Australian Army Major. My ultimate excuse of last resort was "The Squadron Leader won't hear the charge. If you are not happy, confront him about it yourself". No one ever did.

On the other hand, "Jock" kept his promise to "give satisfaction". Some weeks later the Squadron Leader remarked to me:

"Well done with the batman situation, Gooner. Your man Jockass is first class."

Indeed, the Squadron Leader was so pleased with Mulcahy that he refused to release him at the end of Jock's tour of duty.

FOUR
The Mess And Occasional Humour

One of the things I grew to like most about the Squadron Leader was his sense of humour. Sometimes the humour was bizarre, but one always knew it was there, lurking in the depths of the Squadron Leader's eccentric mind.

Early on the Squadron Leader had "ordered" me to stay close to him at all times in the Mess. As a result, I was privy to the social conversations he occasionally had with the Range Commander, General Charles. These conversations would only take place if the General approached the Squadron Leader; indeed I never knew the Squadron Leader to speak to anyone else. Typically the exchanges would be good humoured, with the Squadron Leader joking about the vicissitudes of life. The Squadron Leader always maintained that his upbringing was harsh. The following is typical of the conversations which took place between the two.

General: "Good evening, Charles. What's happening in the world?"

Squadron Leader: "Evening, Bob. All's well. That Commie sot Khrushchev has been at the vodka again. Fell down the steps to some Russian mausoleum drunk as an English Lord" (stretches out hand to pick up a large glass of Johnnie Walker).

General: "Hard times for the Russian leaders these days. No wonder they take to the bottle."

Squadron Leader: "Don't talk to me about hard times. I was brought up in very sorry circumstances."

General: "How so?"

Squadron Leader: "When I was born, my father was sorry; my mother was sorry too. When I was young my parents used to send me to the corner shop to get a newspaper and by the time I got back, they had moved. On my eleventh birthday, my mother asked me what I would like as a present; I said 'something to play with'; she bought me a pair of trousers and cut the pockets out."

General: "You poor sod. Let's go and get you some food before you fade away."

Of course, this was in 1960 and no doubt the jokes have been copied many times since. But at the time I thought them tremendously funny; indeed I had great difficulty in not erupting into loud laughter, which would certainly have brought an icy stare from the Squadron Leader.

I had only been under the Squadron Leader's tender care for a few weeks when his friend the General left, having completed his tour of duty. He was succeeded by an Australian Army Colonel to whom, in his normal way, the Squadron Leader took an instant dislike. The General had always sat at the head of one end of the long dining table, which served the Officers' Mess, with the Squadron Leader next to him on the General's right. Immediately upon the General leaving the Range, the Squadron Leader took over his seat and instructed me to occupy the seat the Squadron Leader had previously occupied. In this way, the Squadron leader sought to avoid talking to anyone at the dining table. He also ordered me to stand four-square in front of him at the bar at all times. He positioned himself at one end of the bar with his back to the wall. If anyone wished to speak to him, they had first to ask me to stand aside. I only remember this happening on four or five occasions and each time the Squadron Leader had moved elsewhere by the time I had moved aside.

FIVE
The Squadron Leader Protects The Good Name Of The Royal Air Force

SAC William Smithson was a minor nuisance. A swaggering type, with a nonchalant air, he was unable to accept discipline. Inevitably he graduated to a major problem.

The first indication I had of difficulties to come commenced with a loud thumping on the Squadron Leader's office door, followed by an even louder blow on my office wall and a roar of "Mr Gooner, come in immediately and bring Mrs Cash with you."

Mrs Cash was a formidable sight. Large and full of aggression. I ushered her into the Squadron Leader's office.

Squadron Leader: "Mrs Cash, the South Australian Police at the guardhouse told me you were on your way to see me. Please have a seat."

Mrs Cash: "I don't want to sit down. I want to know what you're going to do about your airmen coming down to Adelaide with the main objective of getting drunk and taking advantage of our young women."

Squadron Leader: "I am sure that is not true, Mrs Cash, but you must understand that when men have been cooped up here for several months without sight of a lady, it is natural that they should seek female company when on leave. The ship's in port and all that; ha ha."

Mrs Cash: "It's true all right and it's no laughing matter, or won't be when I report your lout Smithson to the South Australian Police."

Squadron Leader: "I know Smithson. Not one of our better men. What offence has he committed, Mrs Cash?"

Mrs Cash: "He has deflowered my daughter and now that she's pregnant he's refusing to have anything to do with it. Are you aware that it is a criminal offence here to deny paternity and to refuse maintenance? Criminal I say; it's not a civil matter."

Squadron Leader: "I am aware, Mrs Cash. Where proven. Are you sure it was Smithson?"

Mrs Cash: "Of course I'm damn well sure. How dare you? If I have to prove it, he will be arrested and the newspapers shall know that you let your wretched men put themselves about in Adelaide."

Squadron Leader (appearing now to be under pressure): "I am sure Smithson is an exception to the good conduct of RAF personnel."

Mrs Cash: "No he's not. I see them frequently snogging and groping our girls in public, in Ewood Park. I think I recognise this one" (points to me). "I am going to take action" (turns to leave).

Squadron Leader: "Calm yourself, Mrs Cash. What is it you would like me to do?"

Mrs Cash: "Tell that lout that he has to marry my daughter."

Squadron Leader: "Leave everything in my hands, Mrs Cash. Smithson will be in Adelaide next weekend all prepared to marry your daughter. Go

Mrs. Cash confronts the Squadron Leader.

back to Adelaide now and make preparations for the wedding." (Turns to me. I am trying to keep a straight face.) "It is beyond my comprehension, Gooner, what you are grinning about. You will accompany SAC Smithson to Adelaide and you will ensure that the marriage takes place and you will report back to me at 09.00 hours on Monday with Smithson, complete with marriage certificate. Any foul-ups are down to you, Gooner. Now ensure Mrs Cash is properly escorted and is able to get a lift on the supply plane back to Adelaide."

I ushered Mrs Cash out.

"Is he always like that?" she asked.

"Always," I replied.

"Please see that useless article gets to us by Friday. I will see you are looked after in Adelaide."

Indeed she did. I was accommodated with her younger sister in more ways than one. The marriage duly took place on Saturday morning at the Registrar's office. As always with Smithson, a problem arose. It appeared that a charge was to be made for issuing the certificate at short notice, plus a supplement for ceremonies on a Saturday. I cannot recall the rates of exchange, but it amounted to £60 sterling (a substantial sum in 1960). To my surprise, Mrs Cash stated firmly and loudly that she had no intention of paying it and the "useless article must pay for something". The fact that Smithson had no more than a few shillings with him did not surprise me. By now you will probably have guessed that I had to lend the money to him and you may have guessed, correctly, that it was never returned.

Upon our return, the marriage certificate was presented to the Squadron Leader, who simply said "dismissed".

A happy day for SAC Smithson.

As we left station headquarters Smithson gritted his teeth and said "The Squadron Leader may have finished with me, but I have not finished with him." I told him not to be stupid and to get back to work. But this was no idle threat from Smithson.

SIX
Smithson Versus The Squadron Leader

Smithson was due to complete his tour of duty and return to his base in England in six months' time, when his wife would be seven months plus pregnant. RAF regulations at that time would not provide passage to England for non-British wives married whilst the husband was on overseas duty. The airfare in 1960 was way beyond Smithson's means. He might have managed to beg, borrow and save enough for a sea passage, but this would have left his wife perilously close to delivering the baby at sea. Smithson therefore took the bull by the horns and made an early request to the Squadron Leader for air passage for his wife on compassionate grounds. The Squadron Leader refused and told him he had a damned cheek to ask.

Smithson knew that there was a loophole in RAF regulations whereby a man relieved of overseas duty and returned home on medical grounds was entitled to be accompanied by his wife. He therefore set about what was commonly referred to as "working his ticket". He assumed that the Squadron Leader would be aware of such tactics; therefore his first effort was by way of testing the water. He tried a well known, if largely unsuccessful, tactic.

The Governor General of South Australia was due to make a rare visit to the Range. A full parade was ordered. All services were present and correct half an hour before the Governor's ETA. The sun blazed down at 35°C. Unfortunately, the Governor's flight was delayed half an hour. Everyone was now very tense. The plane arrived and the Governor stepped onto the tarmac, accompanied by his Secretary and his Air Stewardess. At that moment Smithson broke ranks and ran across the parade ground at high speed.

"Stop that man," bawled the RSM.

"Gooner, get that man," roared the Squadron Leader.

That was not so easy; Smithson was running fast and swerving from side to side. He was eventually collared by an Australian Navy bosun. Smithson was detained in the guardhouse overnight and the RSM brought him before the Squadron Leader next morning, accompanied by my long-suffering self.

Squadron Leader: "Explain yourself, Smithson."

Smithson: "I saw paper, Sir; chasing paper, Sir."

RSM: "Sir, there was no paper. The parade ground was immaculate. This man is mentally unstable, Sir."

Squadron Leader: "Nonsense, Regimental Sergeant Major. I know this man's game. He is looking for early release from his tour of duty. Smithson, you will report to the guardhouse every day after work for the next 14 days. The RSM will arrange a schedule of heavy-duty tasks for you. Dismissed."

When we had left the Squadron Leader called me back in. "Tell Sgt Wilson to keep a very close eye on Smithson on my instructions. He won't be working his ticket on my watch and my watch is going to last for a very long time."

Round One to the Squadron Leader. Round Two saw Smithson running across the screen of the Camp Cinema during an all action cowboy film. He had an empty lemonade bottle in each hand. He turned to face the audience and shouted "Bang, bang, you're all dead, you dirty villains. Lay down and wait for your transport to Boot Hill. Ha, ha, whoopee."

He then rushed out of the cinema, slamming the exit door so hard it sounded like a gunshot from the film. There were, of course, several officers in the front rows. I was sure that the RSM would next morning invoke the usual pantomime of bringing Smithson before the Squadron Leader on a charge. He did not. He marched him straight to the Medical Officer, explained the situations which had occurred and asked the MO to assess Smithson's mental health. The MO had a long talk with Smithson. Later the MO came to see the Squadron Leader and told him that, in his view, Smithson had psychological problems and he would be prepared to declare him unfit for further duty overseas at present, if the Squadron Leader so wished. The Squadron Leader told the MO that he did not so wish and that Smithson was deliberately seeking to be posted back to the UK on medical grounds. The MO was not entirely satisfied and asked for an undertaking that the man would be closely monitored. This undertaking the Squadron Leader gave. Round 2, a draw.

The Squadron Leader then called in Sgt Wilson. I heard every word of the exchange.

Squadron Leader: "I gave you an order to keep that wastrel Smithson under close observation. You have allowed him to run amok around the Range. His latest antics led me into an embarrassing situation with RSM Haskins. What have you to say for yourself?"

Sgt Wilson: "I have tried to keep an eye on him, Sir, but he's unpredictable and I don't think he is suitable for service here."

Squadron Leader: "I don't want your opinion, Sgt Wilson, I simply want you to carry out my orders but you cannot because you are incompetent. Keep that stupid boy fully occupied and keep him away from that halfwit Medical Officer or I'll have your stripes" (shouted very aggressively). "Is that understood?"

Sgt Wilson (loud sounds of coming very smartly to attention): "Yes, Sir."

Squadron Leader: "Get out."

Smithson's final effort came about a week later. The Camp Adjutant made a weekly inspection of other ranks' accommodation on a rota basis. Each unit would be inspected in its turn. The Major would be accompanied by an officer from the unit being inspected and by the RSM, together with two or three corporals. As usual, the Squadron Leader had delegated me to attend the RAF inspection. I dwelt at the back of the inspection column, well out of the firing line. As the Major approached Smithson's hut, I was aware of a very loud shouting and gibbering, very reminiscent of monkey noises. The sound increased as the Major entered. The hut was strewn with dirty clothes and general rubbish. The Major looked around in amazement but saw nothing. The RSM and I did; there was Smithson, crouched low in a monkey posture on top of a wardrobe, making animal noises.

"What are you doing up there?" roared the RSM.

"Climbing a mountain and testing the echo," came back the reply. Then, with one leap, Smithson landed, still on all fours, right in front of the Major.

"Regimental Sergeant Major," said the Adjutant, "this inspection is ended. Follow me to the Medical Centre and bring that wretched fellow with you."

At the Medical Centre the Adjutant informed the Medical Officer that Smithson was mentally deranged and that he be declared unfit for overseas duty.

"I want him off this Range," said the Major.

"So do I," bellowed the RSM.

The Medical Officer interviewed Smithson briefly. The airman explained that he had been making monkey noises to communicate with the Adjutant, who he was certain was a very close member of the primate family; surely the MO understood, was he not a bit of a monkey himself? Mindful of his previous experiences with Smithson, the MO had now heard enough. He told the Adjutant that he concurred. Smithson had been affected by the desert heat and by stress and was unfit for further duty at Maralinga. The Adjutant demanded, and got, a certificate to that effect from the MO.

Normally the Adjutant went in fear of the Squadron Leader's notorious temper, even though the Australian Army Major was equal in rank. Now he was in the ascendancy. He made for Station Headquarters and the Squadron Leader's office straightaway. Here his confidence momentarily deserted him. Nobody was allowed into the Squadron Leader's office without first checking with myself. Even the Range Commander tolerated this diktat. The Major presented himself.

"I must see the Squadron Leader immediately, matter of urgency."

27

Knowing the Squadron Leader was in one of his better moods, I picked up my intercom.

"Gooner here, Sir, the Range Adjutant wishes to see you, a matter most urgent, he says."

"Urgent to him, pain in the butt to me, no doubt. Well, show him in, Goony old chap," (unheard of good humour!) "and let's get rid of him before lunch."

In we go and the Major, confidence suddenly restored, rushes up to the Squadron Leader's desk, thrusting the certificate close to the Squadron Leader's face.

"This is from the Medical Officer; your airman Smithson has cracked up. He must be removed from the Range immediately."

The Squadron Leader stormed from his desk, roaring like a wounded lion.

"How dare you. I am the Commanding Officer of the Royal Air Force Unit on this Range and I alone will decide who is fit for duty, not you or your fellow incompetent the Medical Maniac."

The Adjutant backed off to the door.

"I have the certificate and it is going to the Range Commander with my report. Then we shall see who makes the decisions here; and I thank you not to abuse me and my colleagues any further."

(Beats hasty retreat out of the door as the Squadron Leader hurls a lead crystal glass at him.)

"Better pre-empt the buggers," said the Squadron Leader. "Get a copy of the certificate and I'll attach it with a note on my current report to Edinburgh Fields. Get Sgt Wilson to make advance arrangements for Smithson to be flown back to the UK. Don't tell me, I know, his wife will have to accompany him."

Round 3, victory by knockout, to Smithson.

The Squadron Leader's good humour has now turned 360 degrees into a foul temper. This increases during the afternoon because he is not in the mood to take his usual bottle of Johnnie Walker Black. Late in the afternoon he receives a memo from the Range Commander, referring to the Adjutant's communication about Smithson. He immediately dictates a memo saying that this matter has already been dealt with and suggesting that the Adjutant be instructed to spend his time on more useful matters, e.g. promulgating proper daily Range Standing Orders, instead of interfering with the Commanding Officer of the British Royal Air Force Unit in his dealings with matters concerning his own personnel. Highly satisfied with this rebuff, the Squadron Leader's humour improves. He announces:

"I'm off to my donga for a shave, shit and shower before supper."

In fact I know that he is off to imbibe a large tumbler of his old friend JWB, which he has denied himself all day long.

SEVEN
The Squadron Leader Seeks Female Company

"The Governor General was not satisfied with certain aspects of his recent visit, so he will be returning next Thursday. I want you to be part of the welcoming party upon his arrival at the airfield," the Squadron Leader tells me. "He will be accompanied by his female Secretary and his Air Stewardess. Make sure you bring them to meet me as soon as the Governor General is off on his inspection. Tell them I shall be delighted to show them the Range facilities. Tell them anything but get them here. I need female contact." Gives a loud, coarse laugh, which might be described as dirty.

The Squadron leader must, of course, be obeyed. Accordingly, I joined the airstrip party welcoming the Governor General and his escorts to Maralinga. I wasted no time in conveying to his Secretary and his Air Stewardess the Squadron Leader's invitation to our Station Headquarters and the Range. I presented them to the Squadron Leader. He gave a hideous grin and said:

"How charming to have two gorgeous girls visiting the Range. It will be my pleasure to show you everything. We have an Olympic size pool here; I am sure you will wish to have a swim on a very hot day like this."

The Air Stewardess flashed her eyes at him. "We have no costumes, Sir."

Back came the Squadron Leader: "Not a problem. Underwear is quite acceptable, and I know you young ladies always carry a spare pair of knickers."

"Yes," said the Secretary, "but walking around in a soaking wet bra afterwards is not very comfortable."

The Squadron Leader laughed (not a pleasant sound I assure you). "Anyone can see neither of you need a bra."

I thought the ladies would be offended, but it seemed not. The Squadron Leader produced a half bottle of Johnnie Black and glasses and offered them a drink. I was more than surprised when they accepted. I was not included, of course.

"That will be all, Gooner," was all I got.

I did not see the ladies again, so I am unable to report all that went on that afternoon. I was told that the ladies were lying around the pool, sunbathing in their underwear, for a short while, after which they went off with the Squadron Leader in the general direction of the airstrip. I do know that the Governor General's flight departed on time that afternoon, with the ladies on board.

The Squadron Leader was not seen that afternoon and Sgt Wilson, who wanted some pay forms signed urgently, was unable to find him. Nevertheless, I was taken by surprise when the Squadron Leader did not attend for dinner at the Mess, since this had never happened before. The Colonel enquired after him twice and then announced he would wait no longer and dinner was to be served in ten minutes promptly. I contacted Sgt Wilson by intercom to the Sergeants' Mess and ordered him to get Jock Mulcahy and make a fast and thorough search for the Squadron Leader and told him he would be held responsible if the Squadron Leader missed his evening meal. I then ordered a large Johnnie Black Label in the hope that he would arrive. No sooner had the drink been placed on the bar than Wilson phoned through to say the Squadron Leader had been found and could I come to the cleaning stores as "I cannot deal with the situation". I told the Colonel he had been located and rushed off to the stores. I found Wilson and Jock outside a small room housing expensive materials, which naturally was securely locked. The Squadron Leader could be heard inside, shouting a variety of vile threats and demanding to be let out immediately. I asked Jock to assist me in breaking the door open and we both took running jumps at it, whilst the Squadron Leader roared obscenities from inside.

The door gave way and the Squadron Leader lumbered out.

"How did that happen, Sir?" I asked, fully expecting a long tirade from himself.

"No time to talk about that now," he bellowed. "I've missed my lunch and I'm hungry. Let's get to the Mess before that fool Colonel has the first course removed."

After dinner and several Johnnies, he seemed in very good humour. He told me he had chatted up the ladies, who seemed receptive, so he had manoeuvred them along to the storage room, whereupon they had shoved him in and locked the door. He thought the whole situation was hilarious. I thought – what a carry on!

EIGHT
The Mail Run

Mail for Maralinga was received daily at Watson, a railway halt 26 miles from the Range. A train would halt at some time mid-morning and a separate bag for each service unit would be thrown out. Collection was very parochial. Each unit would send their own Land Rover to collect their mail. Heaven forbid the British Navy should bring back the Australian Army mailbag!

An ancient railway employee occupied a shack at Watson and always kept a large number of canned beers in a canvas bag filled with cold water, for sale to the servicemen.

One morning, at about 08.30, I was slowly making my way to Headquarters through a burning 95F heat when an obviously panic-stricken Sgt Wilson came rushing up to me.

"Sir, some swine has stolen our Jeep and I have nothing to send for the mail. I dare not tell the Squadron Leader. Could you possibly tell him, Sir?"

I adopted a jovial air. "Come now, Sgt, you mustn't be afraid of the Squadron Leader. He is one the most fair-minded men I have ever met."

Wilson's face assumed a sickly grin. "Well, Sir, you are only 21, you won't have seen that many men, and none like the Squadron Leader."

My attitude changed. "Wilson, you lack courage and decision-making ability. Get back to your depressing little office. I shall attempt to rescue you from the consequences of your ineptitude yet again."

I had sent Sgt Wilson scuttling off with his tail between his legs, but, I must confess, I was fearful of the Squadron Leader's reaction.

It occasionally happened that two men would think it a great joke to drive out into the bush with two vehicles, dump one, and return, and a difficult job it would be to find the vehicle. It might even be that another unit, finding their vehicle stolen, had taken ours to get their mail and would dump the Jeep upon return. The Squadron Leader would know all this, of course; but I was unsure how he would react.

The Squadron Leader smiled. "Are there no bicycles?"

"I have never seen a bike on the Range, Squadron Leader."

"That is a pity. There ought to be bicycles available. Better get running then. Think of it as time off for training."

The latter remark was a jibe, concerned with the fact that I boxed regularly in the RAF tournaments and, much to the Squadron Leader's annoyance, I had several times been called off the Range to participate.

"May I ask Sgt Wilson to send a patrol out to look for our Land Rover, Sir?"

"Yes. But in the meantime, set off on foot. I want the mail on my desk before I go to lunch and I am hungry today."

"I will try my best, Sir."

"Don't try, laddie: succeed."

I instructed Sgt Wilson, more in hope than in expectation. I set off at a gentle jog. I felt I could probably manage up to ten miles, by which time I ought to encounter the first of the vehicles coming back. I could flag one down, get a lift back to Watson and return with the mail. By 11:00 I had covered the ten miles; no sign of Wilson, but the wonderful sight of a line of Land Rovers coming towards me. I waved and shouted: no response, except for foul-mouthed abuse. The last of the line passed by. I sank to my knees in despair, my head bowed to the ground. I was alerted by a sudden squeal of brakes and a British Army corporal shouting:

"What the hell's going on? I nearly ran over you."

I explained briefly and, as soon as I reached the part about the Squadron Leader's orders he said: "Say no more, Sir. Jump in, I'll see you right."

Back to Watson we went and I must confess I had a quick beer (extortionate prices, the old bugger was charging). Return to Maralinga and dump the mail on Sgt Wilson and tell him to sort the Squadron Leader's mail and get it to him fast. I return to the Squadron Leader's office and enter, putting on a great show of sweating and gasping for breath.

"Mailbag with Sgt Wilson; your mail with you in a few minutes, Sir."

"Good effort. Worth a drink." The Squadron Leader takes a half bottle of Johnnie Walker from his desk and shakes it at me.

"Thank you, no, Sir. With your permission I will away to the Mess and get a large lemonade."

"Go ahead."

Later I am unable to find Sgt Wilson. When I do catch up with him he tells me:

"I've had to go out into the bush with Jock and a couple of the lads to find the Jeep. Missed lunch and had to bribe Jock to get information. The Squadron Leader called me in and said he thought it fair to warn me he was considering referring me for court marshal for gross negligence resulting in loss of RAF property and that he would review the matter after lunch. I think it is disgraceful, putting me under that kind of pressure."

"Did you recover the Jeep?" I asked.

"Yes."

"What did the Squadron Leader say?"

"He said no further action would be taken on this occasion."

I reflected for a moment, then said:

"You simply don't understand the Squadron Leader. What he was doing was to motivate you to do what you should have done hours ago. Ultimately he has shown leniency and understanding."

Sgt Wilson was obviously still bitter about the incident.

"It is indeed fortunate that you are on the same wavelength as the Squadron Leader, for I am sure no one else is," he muttered as he skulked off. It was probably some kind of dumb insolence, but I was too far-gone to care.

NINE
The Squadron Leader Plays Cricket

My 21st birthday was soon due. Sgt Wilson approached me to say that several of the lads from the RAF and British and Australian Armies had expressed a wish to hold a "Barbie" to celebrate this occasion. I said that I would be very pleased but, as with all things, I would have to clear it with the Squadron Leader. I asked the Squadron Leader if there would be any objections to a small number of men from various services giving a barbecue to celebrate my 21st.

"Out of the question. I am not having RAF personnel involved in a drunken revelry which is sure to get out of control. But your 21st should be marked. Leave it to me. I will arrange something appropriate. Dismissed."

Two days later Sgt Wilson told me he had been instructed to arrange a cricket match; RAF versus Combined Services. The Squadron Leader would captain the RAF.

The Squadron Leader laid down the match rules. 20 overs, no bowler to bowl more than four overs, no more than two men on the boundaries at any time. The Squadron Leader was, of course, 40 years ahead of his time. The Combined Services, led by an Australian Army Lieutenant, won the toss and elected to bat. We took the field with the Squadron Leader as wicketkeeper. They were soon hitting our bowlers all over the place and raced to 120 for 3 off 12 overs. With seven wickets in hand they were sure to hit out for the remaining overs and we looked to be faced with an impossible total of over 200. The Squadron Leader then called Sgt Wilson and me together for a conference.

"You two will bowl the last eight overs. Wilson, I know you will tie them down. Mr Gooner, bowl line and length and no half volleys. You two can turn this game around."

Wilson, unknown to me, had been a good club cricketer. He bowled left handed with his arm behind his back until the last moment. His approach to the wicket mimicked his walking gait; most peculiar. The batsman simply could not hit him. His first over was a maiden. In his second, a frustrated batsman tried to drive and edged an easy catch to slip. His last two overs were the same and, although he gave away two runs, he picked up two more wickets. My first two overs were predictable, fast medium stuff and they picked up 14 runs. The Squadron Leader then called me over.

"Bowl your last two overs down the leg side where they can't touch them."

The Squadron Leader must, of course, be obeyed. I bowled the first three balls wide of the wicket. On the third ball the umpire called "wide". The Squadron Leader stumped slowly across to the official.

"The batsman played at the ball; no wide," he roared and stumped back to the wicket.

"Play," said the umpire.

The next three balls went wide without contact by the batsman or comment from the umpire. The final ball was closer to the stumps. The batsman took a big swipe at it but could only edge it into the Squadron Leader's hands. It was said later that the Squadron Leader's triumphant roar was heard at the Range Forward Area, two miles away. The final over of the innings fell to me. I was confident now and the batsman simply could not make contact with the first five balls. In desperation, the batter lunged at the final ball and gave me the simplest caught and bowled I have ever had. From 120 off 12 overs, they had now finished on 137, a reachable target for us.

In the dressing room the Squadron Leader decided the batting order.

"I will open the batting with Mulcahy. Then Robson, Spearmont and Sgt Wilson in that order. Mr Gooner bats No.11; by then either victory will be his to celebrate or he will have to save the day. The rest of you sort out the order yourselves. Take note of this: I do not run. Do not call for or attempt a run whilst I am at the wicket. Best of luck, lads."

The Squadron Leader took guard at the wicket. His huge bulk completely obliterated the wicket. It would be almost impossible to clean bowl him. Neither umpire would dare give him out lbw. He would not run. The only way he could be out was caught. However, the only ball the Squadron Leader would hit was a loose delivery, which he would simply hit carefully and, aided by his enormous weight, it would crash to the boundary. Slowly the Squadron Leader amassed runs. The problem lay in the fact that the Squadron Leader would not run, therefore the others could not. Runs had to come by boundaries. The batsmen were tempted to lash out and the early wickets fell quickly. Jock Mulcahy, John Robson and Billy Spearmont all fell within six overs, with the total at 24 runs. Sergeant Wilson then came in and played a cautious game, defending his wicket and gathering the occasional four, with the Squadron Leader averaging two fours each over he faced. Thus they proceeded until the score reached 102 after 14 overs. We were nearly on target to win. Then it was that Wilson forgot his instructions. Hitting a glorious cover drive, he set off to run. He was ten yards down the wicket before he realised that the Squadron Leader had not moved. Desperately he scrambled back, to no avail. It was a simple run out. The next five batsmen were out within four overs, contributing only eight runs. The Squadron Leader continued to hit two fours each over, so that I came in as last man at 126, with two overs remaining and 12 runs required to win.

The Squadron Leader met me mid-wicket and growled, "Remember, no running."

I had three balls to face. Our opponents had sensibly left their two fast bowlers to finish the final overs. I never really saw any of these last three balls. Two shot past me but did not hit the wicket. The third one I stopped with my thigh. Up went the roar "Owzat". The Squadron Leader took two paces down the wicket and assumed his "very annoyed" face.

"Not out," said the umpire. The Squadron Leader faced the final over from which we would have to get 12 runs without running. The first ball flew at our Captain at around 85mph. He simply pushed his bat at it in a straight line and it shot past the bowler, nearly taking his legs off, and onto the boundary for four. The bowler then cannily bowled the next three wide of the wicket. The first two the Squadron Leader could not move quickly enough to get to. The next ball he moved across the wicket just before the bowler released the ball, thus he was able to reach it and, although it was not a clean shot, it raced away for four. The fifth ball was a short bouncer to which the Squadron Leader could only duck. Final ball and four wanted. The bowler hurled down a fast, short-pitched ball. The Squadron Leader stretched as far forward as possible but could not reach the ball, which sailed over his head. Game over and a win for Combined Services surely? But no! Stretching so far forward had caused the Squadron Leader to let out a thunderclap of a fart. Startled by the sound and overpowered by the stench of the Johnnie Walker and scrambled eggs mixture, the wicketkeeper staggered to the left. The ball went straight through to the boundary. Four runs; we have won and the Squadron Leader is the hero. Several team members attempt to hoist him shoulder high in triumph. Alas, the Squadron Leader's weight proves too much, even for six stalwart men. They all crash to the ground with the Squadron Leader on top. Chaos reigns again.

We retire to the changing room. The Squadron Leader produces four bottles of Johnnie Walker Black Label. I do not drink, but the rest of the team get drunk. I recall the Squadron Leader's original comments to me. I reflect that whatever the outcome, the Squadron Leader is, of course, always correct.

The Victory Hoist for the Squadron Leader crashes.

TEN
Walkabout

About 50 miles north of Maralinga lay one of the largest Aboriginal reservations of the 1960s era. Frequently an Aborigine would leave the reservation and go "walkabout", usually with a young girl in tow. On these occasions the Range Commander would be asked to send a party out to recover the recalcitrant. Each unit would take its turn to perform this duty. Inevitably the turn of the British RAF came around.

"I shall lead the party, Gooner," said the Squadron Leader. "Round up a few likely lads, but for heaven's sake don't bring Sgt Wilson. My blood pressure is high enough already without his imbecility adding to it."

We are assembled. The Squadron Leader takes charge.

"We will proceed first to the reservation and get the up-to-date information from the agent there. Mulcahy to drive." At the reservation we are told that the Aborigine has been gone for about four hours. He is fortyish, nicknamed "Charlie" and has taken a thirteen-year-old girl with him. He has at least one throwing spear and a war boomerang.

The Squadron Leader considers the problem.

"He won't have gone south towards the Range and we might have spotted him anyway. He won't have gone north towards the mosquitoes. East is much more isolated than west. The east it is then. With the girl to slow him down, he won't have gone much more than 15 miles. We will take a circle of 20 miles in radius and come in with decreasing circles. Shouldn't take long to catch him."

As always, the Squadron Leader is right. We completed one full circle without success but, halfway through the second circle, we spotted "Charlie" and the girl. We drive to within 100 yards, stop and dismount. The Aborigine makes no attempt to run. He stands very still, two spears in this right hand and a heavy hardwood boomerang in his left hand. The girl is directly behind him.

The Squadron Leader addresses "Charlie" in some form of pigeon English. The gist of it is that "Charlie" should come forward to the Land Rover, where we have food and drink for him and the girl. "Charlie" replies by hurling a spear at the Squadron Leader's head. For once the Squadron Leader's vertically challenged frame is beneficial; the spear brushes the top of his head. The Squadron Leader speaks:

"Flt Lt Gooner, take Phillips and circle to the right. Walker, you and Stevens circle to the left. Come together and trap the Aborigine."

Phillips and I close in on one flank and Walker and Stevens on the other. The Aborigine is well aware of what is happening. He waits until we have almost completed the pincer movement and then, leaving the girl, he rushes straight ahead. Only the Squadron Leader bars his way. He throws the boomerang at the Squadron Leader and swerves to the left. The Squadron Leader takes one half pace to the right; the Aborigine crashes into him and is knocked backwards, flat on his back. Walker, Stevens and Phillips pounce and secure him. The girl has tried to run, but finds me blocking her path. She stops, smiles and holds out her hand, which I take and gently lead her back to the Land Rover. The Squadron Leader leers lasciviously. "Trust you to get the girl, Gooner."

We return to the reservation. The agent is delighted and offers drinks: "Only cactus juice, but it's a good, strong, alcoholic brew". The lads go for it greedily. I explain that I do not drink as I am in training and that the Squadron Leader drinks only Johnnie Walker Black Label. An enormous grin comes over the agent's face. "Perhaps you would like to join me, Sir," he says, producing a bottle of Johnnie Black.

"Where the devil did that come from?" roars the Squadron Leader.

"Always keep a bottle for medicinal purposes. Eases the cactus juice constipation," says the agent, giving an outrageous wink. The agent and the Squadron Leader set to and it is an hour before we can leave the reservation.

We return to the Range with the Squadron Leader in good humour. He has kept the boomerang, which is in teak wood and beautifully carved with symbols to represent the story of "Charlie's" life and his dreams. It is rather special and the Squadron Leader has kept it to this day. Indeed, I saw it again quite recently.

Waiting at the Range is a message for the Squadron Leader, asking him to contact the Range Commander as a matter of urgency. It seems that an electrical contact unit had been required immediately and, in the Squadron Leader's absence, the Range Commander had signed the requisition. This had been presented to Sgt Wilson, who promptly said he would not be able to identify where a spare unit was stored. This was relayed to the Commander, who told Wilson to fetch the inventory ledgers to him (everything was kept in handwritten books and cards in those days). The Range Commander was unable to locate the item in the lists and Sgt Wilson compounded matters by saying that he knew nothing of the ledgers as the Squadron Leader had said he was incompetent and should not touch them. The Range Commander adopted a very nasty attitude with the Squadron Leader, saying that the two RAF officers should not both be off the Range at the same time and that an NCO, who was known to the Squadron Leader as being incompetent, should not have been left in charge of the RAF Unit. For once the Squadron Leader was unable to reply. He did, of course, vent his fury on Sgt Wilson.

"You really are an idiot, Sergeant. Why did you not tell the Range Commander that the ledgers were kept locked away for security and only myself and Flt Lt Gooner had the keys?"

"Well, because that's not true, Sir."

"Good grief, man. Did you not consider that by telling the Commander that only Mr Gooner and I had the key, you could have immediately sent someone out to collect Mr Gooner and bring him back?"

"I didn't think, Sir."

"Of course you didn't. You are incapable of thinking. Dismissed."

"Oh, before I forget, Sir, the Mess Steward was trying to deliver a package to you but was unable to find you. He would have gone away, but I told him to leave it with me" (produces a brown paper bag).

"Wilson, you never cease to amaze me. You intersperse slow-wittedness with quick thinking. I never know when I am going to suffer the burden of one or gain the benefit of the other." Squadron Leader grabs the bag. "All's well that ends well. I'm off to my donga until suppertime, Mr Gooner."

ELEVEN
Time For Leave

The Squadron Leader had not taken any leave during my time on the Range, so it was no surprise when he called me into his office and announced that he was taking seven days' leave in Adelaide. He would take a lift in the next supply plane returning from the Range.

"Would you like me to ask Sgt Wilson to arrange accommodation, Sir?"

"No thank you. I shall be staying with Mrs Cash. Don't look so surprised, we have been corresponding ever since Smithson and her daughter were returned to the UK with my kind permission. We are desirous of meeting under more favourable circumstances. Tell Mulcahy to take leave; that will be convenient for me."

I must say my first reaction was amazement. On reflection, I considered that they were both large and aggressive and heavy drinkers, so they might get on well together. Their problem and, hopefully, not mine.

Any thoughts I had that I would be relieved of problems with the Squadron Leader were naïve. On the third day of his leave, the Squadron Leader telephoned me from Adelaide.

"How are things going in my absence, Mr Gooner?"

"All quiet and in order, Sir."

"Any problems with the imbecile?"

"No, Sir. Sgt Wilson hasn't raised any problems with me, Sir."

"Sounds suspicious to me; keep an eye on him."

"Are you enjoying your leave, Squadron Leader?"

"I am not, Goony. I have problems down here."

As soon as I hear the Squadron Leader address me in familiar terms I know that I am going to be confronted with some personal predicament.

"What is the problem, Squadron Leader?"

"Problems, I said, Goony, in the plural. I am not getting on with Mrs Cash so I shall have to find some other accommodation. She runs a tight ship here; too many rules and regulations for my liking. Also she is a very heavy drinker, which makes her subject to extreme mood changes. I have to go somewhere but where I am not sure."

"And the other problems, Squadron Leader?"

"I have run out of Johnnie Black" (I know he took three bottles with him) "and I cannot find anywhere that stocks it. Furthermore, you will understand that, given my long spell on the Range, together with the fiasco with the Governor General's ladies, I am much in need of female company and I do not mean the lush Mrs Cash. What am I do to, Goony?"

I was quite concerned. Normally the Squadron Leader treated me as though I was "wet behind the ears" (his expression). He would never ask my advice, but now he was asking for it. Some quick thinking was called for.

"Squadron Leader, I believe you could solve all three problems with one action. You could book into the Queen's Hotel. I have stayed there and found the accommodation and staff first rate. Johnnie Walker is available at the Residents' Bar, so I am sure the barman could get some supplies for you. Also the head waitress, Gladys, is a mature and most charming lady, very much to your taste, I should think, Sir."

"Goony, I feel you are progressing well under my tuition. Well done, young sir."

I did not inform the Squadron Leader that Jock Mulcahy was staying at the Queen's Hotel, but I did telephone Jock to alert him to the situation.

It was several days after the Squadron Leader's return before I learnt something of his adventures in Adelaide. This I pieced together from what Gladys and Jock told me and from the Squadron Leader himself.

Jock was on hand to greet the Squadron Leader upon his arrival and was able to tell him that the barman had two bottles of Johnnie Black in hand and had ordered a case of a dozen to be delivered. The Squadron Leader was now in great good humour and invited Jock to have a drink with him. They were served by Gladys and the Squadron Leader quickly fell into conversation with her. As I had predicted, they got on very well together. So much so, that Gladys agreed to spend the next two days showing the Squadron Leader the best of Adelaide's beautiful city.

The first morning was spent rowing on the River Torrens. Gladys said that the Squadron Leader was a very powerful rower and they soon reached the quieter stretches of the river where they moored up and indulged in a wonderful picnic hamper, which the Squadron Leader had ordered at the hotel. The Squadron Leader had his flask of Johnnie Walker with him and thus it was that Gladys drank most of a bottle of champagne. This caused her to be most affectionate towards the Squadron Leader, which seemed to take him greatly by surprise. Back on dry land the afternoon was spent at Ewood Park and they were fortunate enough to catch a military band playing in the splendid amphitheatre. The Squadron Leader, continuing to be fortified by his flask, was in grand form, croaking along to several songs. Later they went to a cocktail bar, which the Squadron Leader described as "outrageously expensive". From there to an upmarket restaurant, where the Squadron Leader said the food was very good, but the prices were "scandalous" and their failure to stock Johnnie Walker Black "deplorable". Since Gladys had to do two hours' night relief work, it was then a taxi back to the hotel.

They spent the next day together at Port Noarlunga. The Squadron Leader was stimulated by the sight of the long sandy beach, swept by the awesome waves of the Southern Ocean where it met the Gulf of St Vincent, so much so that he decided to go for a swim. Gladys said she would sit on the beach and watch, but the grotesque sight of the Squadron Leader stripped down to his shorts was too much for her and she departed to wait for him in the nearby hotel. Despite the blazing sun, the Squadron Leader was still very wet when he returned. He wanted to book a room so that they could "share some private time together". Gladys dissuaded him on the grounds that she was working later that evening, but to pacify him she put him on a promise for the following evening, when she would be free.

The next day would be the Squadron Leader's last day on leave as he had to catch an early flight the following day. He spent the early part of the day watching cricket at the Adelaide Oval, even taking a few beers and wallowing in blissful anticipation of the night to come. He returned to the Queen's Hotel to find a message from Gladys saying she had some things to do in the early evening and suggesting they meet at the Vesuvius Nightclub. On arrival, he was extremely annoyed to see Gladys seated at a table, accompanied by two other gentlemen. However, Gladys greeted him effusively, kissed him passionately and poured him a glass of champagne from a magnum in an ice bucket. Mollified by this, the Squadron Leader allowed himself to be introduced to Gladys's friends and to have his glass replenished. It appeared the party had eaten earlier and, much to the Squadron Leader's annoyance, the nightclub only served hors d'oeuvres. Determined to make a good impression on Gladys, the Squadron Leader said nothing about the food and ordered more champagne. Dancing began but the Squadron Leader refused to partake. Instead he continued drinking and, upon being told Johnnie Walker was not available, he decided to stick to champagne and ordered more.

The champagne flowed out and at some point during the evening the Squadron Leader fell asleep (he says; Gladys says he passed out), to be awakened by Gladys telling him it was 1am, handing him the bill and telling him it was time to go. They went to Gladys's flat, where she suggested she give him coffee to sober him up. Whilst she was making it, the Squadron Leader was violently sick and then passed out. With the help of the porter and a cab driver, she managed to get him into a taxi and back to the Queen's Hotel. Here, with the help of the hotel porter and the night barman, the Squadron Leader was manhandled up to this room. I have not been able to establish who undressed him, but a naked Squadron Leader was roused at 6am by the hotel porter, who reminded him that he had to get the 7am flight from Edinburgh Fields. Somehow the Squadron Leader made it. During the flight to Maralinga, the Squadron Leader was plagued with a ferocious headache and was sick three times.

The Squadron Leader arrived in what was obviously a foul mood. Maralinga was a restricted area and certain items were prohibited from being brought onto the Range. An NCO from the Royal Australian Air

Force was always on duty when any aircraft landed on the airstrip.

"Anything to declare, Sir?"

The Squadron Leader ignored him and walked straight on. The NCO chased after him and laid a restraining hand on his shoulder. The Squadron Leader stopped, turned and gave the NCO a ferocious stare.

"I am Squadron Leader Folly, Officer Commanding Royal Air Force. If you seek to detain me any further I shall have you court marshalled for laying hands on a Senior Officer and obstructing his passage."

The Squadron Leader strode on. The NCO shouted: "I don't give a damn who you are. Have you anything to declare?"

Fortunately Jock Mulcahy was a few paces behind and spoke quietly to the NCO: "Leave it, mate. He won't hesitate to put you on a charge and no one is going to argue against him."

When the Squadron Leader arrived at headquarters, I could tell he was not feeling well.

"Are you alright, Sir?"

"No, Mr Gooner, I have a stinking hangover. I shall sit quietly in my office this afternoon. See that I am not disturbed."

Until that time I had never known the Squadron Leader to have a hangover. I left him in peace, but took the initiative of informing the Mess Steward that he had returned. At about 4pm I heard the crash of bottle against wall and the heavy tread of the Squadron Leader departing. All was back to normal.

TWELVE
Woomera Hosts The Squadron Leader

It was 08:25 and the sun was blazing, with the temperature already in the 90s. I was hurrying to headquarters in the hope of arriving before the Squadron Leader. No chance. As I approach my cubby hole I hear the Squadron Leader is already banging on the wall with his staff. I go straight to his office door and knock.

"Gooner here, Sir."

"Come in, my boy" (once again I am cautious in the face of such unusual familiarity).

The Squadron Leader is looking particularly pleased with himself.

"I am going to Woomera next weekend and I want you to hold the fort and see that the jackass" (Sergeant Wilson) "does nothing stupid."

"Why Woomera, Sir?" I ask.

"Our rugby team are playing matches there and I am going to write the match reports for the Range Magazine."

Maralinga had a good rugby team, which won most of their matches. I was not a fan. I was contemptuous of the vicious fouling on the blind side of the referee, which seemed to be an integral part of the game. Another ritual of the matches, which I detested, was the drunken hooliganism which followed every game and which invariably lasted into the early hours of the morning. I once complained bitterly about the nighttime noise to the Squadron Leader. His reply was:

"Just sportsmen winding down after a hard match; no cause for complaint there."

The Squadron Leader was a keen rugby follower who had played as a prop forward in this prime, so I quite understood his following the team to Woomera.

The Squadron Leader continued:

"You have been to Woomera on these boxing jollies of yours. Tell me about the place."

"You will be at Woomera Village, Sir, which is the domestic support site for the Nurringer Missile Test Range. About 7,000 personnel, of which 4,000 are in married quarters."

The Squadron Leader stirred impatiently.

"I know all that. Don't waste my time. What goes on up there, is there any fun to be had? Can I get Johnnie or do I need to take it with me?"

I chose my words carefully.

"There are about 2,000 women living in the Village, mostly married. The main form of entertainment at the weekends is open house; you will find about 200 houses where a party is going on. The front doors are left open and people wander from one house to another, having a couple of drinks and dancing or singing at each. It is accepted practice that people consort with each other, regardless of marital status. It is expected that you bring a few beers to every house you visit."

"What about Johnnie?"

"Sir, there is a general store that sells alcohol, but I should think that something as special as Johnnie Walker Black Label would have to be ordered in advance. Shall I ask Sergeant Wilson to phone ahead and order, say, four bottles?"

"Good God, no. If Wilson has anything to do with it, I will end up with Black Label brand Walking Kit. Deal with it yourself, Goony."

I was glad to be rid of the Squadron Leader for a few days, but my gain was certainly Woomera's punishment. Relieved of the burden of office, the Squadron Leader's behaviour might euphemistically be described as excessively euphoric. Various tales filtered back; none more interesting than his exploits on his second night at Woomera.

After visiting two or three houses, an inebriated Squadron Leader found himself dancing in a small, and thus very crowded, front room. Inevitably his huge bulk crashed into several people, until he was asked not to dance. The Squadron Leader took hold of his dancing partner and found a seat, placing her upon his lap. Unfortunately her husband appeared almost immediately.

"That's my wife. You'd better come outside with me, Pommie."

The Squadron Leader, not quite sure what was happening, followed him. Once outside, the outraged husband wasted no time but immediately hit the Squadron Leader with a right-hander to the head. This resulted in a shooting pain all the way up the assailant's right arm and he knew

55

immediately that his hand was broken. Trying to save face he said,

"Let that be a lesson to you."

The Squadron Leader, aware only of a buzzing sensation in the head, which he normally associated with Johnnie Black, said "Most certainly" and staggered on to the next house. After a couple of cans of lager there he felt the need to relieve himself. Asking direction to the bathroom, he was told:

"Upstairs, first on the right, cobber."

Whether the informant did not know his left from his right, was drunk or plain mischievous, is not known. Mounting the stairs and opening the right-hand door, the Squadron Leader found himself in a bedroom, with the bed occupied by two clearly drunken ladies lying in each other's arms. The Squadron Leader began to apologise profusely. One lady sat up in the bed, displaying all her ample charms.

"Why don't you come and join us?" she said. The Squadron Leader, being a gentleman of the old school, could never refuse a lady.

The Squadron Leader awoke to find himself alone, lying upon the floor, underneath a window. Gathering himself together, he looked for the two things he always sought first thing in the morning: his flask of Johnnie Black and his wallet. He could find neither. Staggering downstairs, he encountered a very large lady, whom he vaguely remembered from the previous night.

"Madam," he said, "I awoke in strange circumstances, lying on the floor of your bedroom, under a window."

"Well," said the large lady, "you weren't doing anything useful in our bed, so we tipped you out onto the floor. You then started to snore like a demented gorilla, so we rolled you over to the window, as far from us as possible."

"That's all very well, but I cannot find my hip flask or my wallet," roared the Squadron Leader.

"Don't shout at me," the lady replied. "I have your flask. I washed it out for you."

The Squadron Leader's face turned a whiter shade of pale.

"It was filled with Johnnie Walker Black Label whisky," he moaned.

"Is that what it was," said the lady. "Vile smelling stuff. I flushed it away before washing it."

The Squadron Leader groaned. "Have you seen my wallet?"

"No," said the lady, "but you had obviously paid several visits before you arrived here. It could be anywhere. Check with the police station and clear off before my husband gets home."

The Squadron Leader was in no mood for further confrontations and took himself off to the police station. As soon as he explained the loss of his wallet, the Squadron Leader was directed to a large room, which contained many dozens of trays filled with wallets.

"Last night's hand-ins and litter pick up are at the front on the left; have a look through them yourself," said the police sergeant.

The Squadron Leader quickly found his wallet; it was, needless to say, empty of cash, but, more importantly, his identity card was missing. The Squadron Leader was now in a foul mood so, of course, he telephoned me. His instructions were for me to retrieve his spare identity card – a belt and braces man, the Squadron Leader, and boy did he need them – and to meet him at the Maralinga airstrip the next day. In the meantime he would spend the rest of the day preparing his report on the rugby matches and I should tell the Range Magazine editor to hold the front page.

Next morning I attended duty at the airstrip. The Squadron Leader duly arrived and, when I saw the thunderous look on his face, I knew that anyone who crossed his path was likely to become very sorry for themselves. The usual security guard was on duty:

"Identification, please, Sir."

"I have lost my identification card, but my second-in-command has a replacement," replied the Squadron Leader.

I leaned across the guard and handed the duplicate to the Squadron Leader. The guard examined it.

"It is not signed," he said arrogantly. The Squadron Leader sailed on; over his shoulder he shouted,

"Don't worry, you wouldn't be able to read my signature anyway."

The guard chased after him.

"Anything to declare?" he bawled.

"Go to hell," roared the Squadron Leader and clambered into the Jeep which I had brought. "Get me out of here and away from this imbecile now," he shouted at me.

I drove off at once and, to my utter amazement, the Squadron Leader regaled me all the way back with hilarious tales of various characters he had encountered at Woomera. I reflected upon how nice it was to have the Squadron Leader back again.

THIRTEEN
The Forward Area Greets The Squadron Leader

The Nuclear Guided Missile Testing Area at Maralinga was set up as a separate specialist unit in the desert, about five miles north of the Service Unit at Maralinga Range. It housed some highly valuable parts and equipment and it fell within my remit to check the inventory on site at least once a year.

The appropriate time came around and I reported to the Squadron Leader that I would be going to the forward area for two days.

"No, Mr Gooner. I shall go myself. I have not visited them and I should like to see what goes on up there."

I wanted to see the forward area myself, so I thought it was worth one try to put the Squadron Leader off.

"I believe it is very dry up there, Sir."

"Don't try to teach your Squadron Leader to suck eggs, laddie. I shall take my own supplies. Tell the Jockass to stand by."

The next morning the Squadron Leader set off in the Land Rover, with Jock at the wheel. Arriving at the Testing Area, they were met by an Australian Army guard. After giving his personal details and the reason for his visit, the Squadron Leader waited whilst the guard checked for authority to allow entry. The guard returned.

"All in order, Sir. May I check your holdall, Sir?"

The Squadron Leader spoke very slowly.

"I am a Senior Officer. There is no need to check my personal effects."

"All baggage must be checked before entry onto this Area is permitted," said the guard.

The Squadron Leader handed over his valise and sat sulking. Upon inspecting the case, the guard removed two bottles of Johnnie Walker.

"No alcohol permitted on this site, Sir. These items will be confiscated in accordance with site regulations," said the guard.

The Squadron Leader leapt from the Land Rover and roared:

"How dare you speak to a Senior Officer in that manner. Get your Duty Officer here immediately."

Casually the guard went to his intercom and made a call, which the Squadron Leader could not hear, but which he felt certain contained abusive references to himself. An Australian Naval Lieutenant arrived and the Squadron Leader straightaway let forth with a tirade of complaints and demands.

"This Corporal has failed to salute me; does not stand to attention when addressing me; and has stated that he has confiscated some of my personal possessions. This man must be placed on charges immediately. I am here to carry out an unannounced inventory check. I require an escort to your equipment warehouse and personnel to assist me with my inspection. I also require refreshments and I wish to inspect the accommodation for myself and my orderly."

The Lieutenant was clearly staggered by this onslaught, but, in true naval fashion, quickly pulled himself together. Taking one pace towards the Squadron Leader, he spoke firmly:

"No alcohol allowed in this area. Your personal property will be held here and returned to you when you leave. I have no visitors' accommodation available, but I have an army private on leave, so you can use his hut and I will arrange a camp bed for your man to share with one of the other ranks. If you will proceed along this road and turn left at the bottom, you will find the stock compound; there are two storekeepers there who will assist you. Lunch is in 45 minutes; it is nothing much and we all eat together here. Good day to you. Carry on Corporal" (salutes and marches off swiftly).

The Squadron Leader screams after him, "The Range Commander shall hear of your insolence, cretin."

The Lieutenant ignores him, knowing, as everyone at Maralinga does, that the Range Commander and the Squadron Leader detest each other.

The Squadron Leader turns to Jock. "Drive on, Mulcahy. You will assist me with the stock check. We must finish today. I am not staying on this ill-organised and undisciplined site overnight."

Jock drove to the bottom of the road and pulled up.

"Left, man, left," roared the Squadron Leader.

"Just a moment, Sir, I need something from my kitbag." Jock produces a half bottle of Johnnie Walker Black Label. "Emergency supplies, Sir. They were too busy with your bag to check mine."

The Squadron Leader beamed. "Jock, you are a treasure. You must continue working for me when we both finish our service." Jock's reply was inaudible and unprintable.

They arrived at the warehouse. Jock pushed the door open to admit the Squadron Leader. A large tin tray, which had been propped against the door, crashed to the ground, making a thunderous noise. An Army Private came rushing out of a cubicle at the rear of the store.

"What is going on here?" roared the Squadron Leader. He rushed past the bemused Private and into the rear cubicle. Here he found two Able Seamen and a Senior Aircraftsman hastily gathering up cards and money from a storage box table.

"Who is in charge here?" shouted the Squadron Leader.

"I am, Sir," came back from the Senior Aircraftsman.

"What are you two doing here?" the Squadron Leader asked the two naval ratings.

"We are off duty, Sir," said one.

"Get out," bawled the Squadron Leader. Turning to the Senior Aircraftsman, the Squadron Leader yelled, "You are in trouble, laddie. I am here to carry out a random inventory check. Get your record cards and ledgers out immediately. Get some overalls for my airman, tell that Private he is improperly dressed and have him stand by to take out items for my inspection."

The store man explained that all records were now kept on a machine –

an early forerunner of a computer – which had recently been purchased. The Squadron Leader was furious, as he had known nothing of this. The inspection proceeded with the Private handing down samples for the Squadron Leader's scrutiny: the storekeeper calling out totals from the machine screen and Jock counting quantities. The occasional discrepancy brought forth garbled explanations from the store man in computer speak. It was now close to lunchtime and the Squadron Leader's mind could not assimilate this nonsense. Fortunately a loud siren wailed, saving the storekeeper from further difficulties. The Squadron Leader was told this meant lunch would be served in five minutes.

"Got to wash my hands, Jock. Where's my toilet bag?" The Squadron Leader was handed the bag, which included the half bottle of Johnnie Black. The Squadron Leader was a few minutes late to the lunch table and the smell of whisky was unmistakable. The Duty Officer was visibly annoyed.

"We start lunch on time here; you're late," he said.

The Squadron Leader snorted. "Not my fault if you delay me because you haven't got anybody who can add up so you give control to machines."

"Our machine is wholly reliable," spluttered the Duty Officer. "It is manual records that suffer from human fallibility; you need a computer."

The Squadron Leader roared, "I am a qualified accountant. I don't need a machine to calculate for me."

"Let's get on with lunch, shall we?" said the Duty Officer.

"If you call this rubbish lunch then you get on with it," said the Squadron Leader, getting up and walking out and making a lot of noise doing it.

Back at the warehouse, the Squadron Leader announced he was going to the office cubicle to consider what to do about the discrepancies. He told Jock to carry on with the stock take. About two hours later Jock went to look for the Squadron Leader and found him sitting peacefully with a big smile on his face. The half bottle was, of course, empty.

"Mulcahy, let us depart from this shambolic place," said the Squadron Leader.

They drove to the guardhouse. Here the Squadron Leader demanded that the Duty Officer be called. The Officer arrived, clearly in a bad temper at being called away from his duties.

"I am signing off the Inspection Form," said the Squadron Leader, "but I will be back."

The Duty Officer's face twisted into a sardonic smile. "Presumably that will be when you have got a computer?"

"Drive on, Mulcahy," snarled the Squadron Leader.

Arriving back at the Range, they found Sgt Wilson in a state of panic. "I have to dispatch the payroll figures tomorrow, Sir, and we cannot reconcile the account. Some of these airmen they are sending me now cannot even add up." This struck a jarring note with the Squadron Leader.

"Obviously there is some simple error. There is no need to panic. You have all night to find and correct it. Let Mr Gooner know when you have done so and see me first thing in the morning."

Much to my annoyance I was woken at 1am by Sgt Wilson, who was pleased to inform me that the payroll had been reconciled. I told him to bugger off, at which he was most offended, and good luck to him.

Reporting to the Squadron Leader next morning, Sgt Wilson was informed that he needed some form of mechanised accounting system. "You mean a computer, Sir?" said Wilson.

"I don't care what it is bloody well called," roared the Squadron Leader, "raise an indent to Edinburgh Field and get one here sharpish and cease continuously wasting my time."

The computer was duly ordered and an object the size of a filing cabinet soon arrived. The Squadron Leader immediately called Sgt Wilson in and told him: "The utmost use must be made of this machine. I want no more failure to reconcile figures due to the idleness and ineptitude of your team. You can start by double-checking these stock figures which have been produced by Mr Gooner as though he were producing a diseased rabbit out of a hat."

Sgt Wilson was so pleased with the arrival his new toy that he was not annoyed by this tirade. It took about a week for something to go wrong.

Sgt Wilson reported that the computer kept cutting out and flagging up a message "no signal". The Squadron Leader questioned why he was being told. "Do you need me to tell you to get an engineer up from Edinburgh Field?" he asked.

"No, Sir," was the standard reply from the Sergeant.

"Then get on with it, you incompetent," came the standard, full volume retort from the Squadron Leader.
The engineer duly arrived and, after about two hours of inspecting and

testing, he reported to the Squadron Leader.

"Can't do anything with this. These machines are a new invention and they're very sensitive. The temperature is over 90°F here. This machine is overheating. It needs a small, air-conditioned office."

The Squadron Leader's face was grim. "We have no air-conditioned facilities on the Range." His voice reminded me of a knife plunged into solid ice.

"No problem," said the engineer. "I can get you a portable unit and fix a ventilator through to an outside wall. Just tell me where you want it."

The Squadron Leader roared: "Why didn't you say so straightaway, instead of wasting my time? It will have to go into the office next to mine."

I was most alarmed. "That is my cubby hole, Sir, where am I to work?"

"Not sure I would call what you've been doing work. There is a spare desk in my office that you can have in the mornings and you can spend the afternoons out and around the Range, checking the inventory, which is what you should have been doing these past months."

I noticed Sgt Wilson grinning. "What is your problem, Sergeant?" I enquired.

"Nothing, Sir, just visualising myself using the computer in the air-conditioned room, whilst you are closeted with the Squadron Leader."

"Very well, Sgt Wilson, I shall bear in mind your sense of humour when such is required in abundance for some unpleasant task."

Sgt Wilson ceased to grin.

The air-conditioning unit was installed a few days later. The Squadron Leader came in to inspect. The temperature was well over 100°F outside. The computer was humming merrily away in a fresh temperature of 65°F. The Squadron Leader smiled – a horrible sight – saying, "What fool said men were smarter than machines?" He turned and left.

FOURTEEN
The Squadron Leader Thinks He Is Funny

I was now ensconced in the Squadron Leader's office every morning and was privy, amongst other things, to his unique brand of humour. This mainly revealed itself in exchanges with the Range Adjutant, Major Wallis, and our rather dopey Sgt Wilson.

One day the Squadron Leader arrived late – something I had never known to happen – and with his head bandaged.

"What has happened, Sir?" I made the obligatory enquiry.

"Our numbskull Adjutant has had a wooden box installed halfway up the wall outside the RSM's office and I walked headfirst into it. Worse still, I have required attention from the Medical Maniac. I now require complete tranquillity for the rest of today and I rely on you, Gooner, to ensure that I get it."

"Of course, Sir. I will remain in the office today to ensure you are not disturbed."

At lunchtime I had the opportunity to see what had caused the Squadron Leader such pain. On the floor outside the RSM's office lay some smashed pieces of wood, together with a sign stating "ideas box". The next day a new box was fixed to the wall and all sections received a memorandum from the Adjutant informing them that ideas for improvements in administration of the Range would be welcome from any service or rank. Later that week, at supper, the Adjutant was bemoaning the fact that there had been very little response to his "ideas" initiative. He addressed himself to the Squadron Leader.

"I am particularly disappointed with your RAF laddies. I thought the Brylcreem Boys were supposed to be a bright bunch."

"I believe our men have had some thoughts," said the Squadron Leader; "problem is, I have forbidden them to suggest anything that might be construed as personal abuse towards the Station Adjutant." Here the Squadron Leader paused and then continued, "There is enough of that sort of thing going on already."

The next day the Squadron Leader put a note into the ideas box which said "Why not two boxes? If an idea is worth having once, it is worth having twice." That afternoon a second box was installed, alongside the new box, at a height of exactly five feet. Reporting for work the next morning I noticed that both boxes were smashed down and lying in pieces outside the RSM's door. As I have said, the Squadron Leader's brand of humour was unique. Later that morning I answered a loud knock on the door to find the Adjutant asking to see the Squadron Leader. Conscious of the Squadron Leader's demand for tranquillity, I said that he was busy at present. The Squadron Leader interrupted me.

"Come in, dear boy, come on in. Whatever is the matter?"

"My ideas boxes have been smashed up," snarled the Adjutant.

Smiling broadly, the Squadron Leader said, "Someone obviously had the wrong idea."

A good deal of the Squadron Leader's version of humour consisted of sarcasm directed at Sgt Wilson. The following is a small selection of conversations between the two, which I can assure you always ended with the Squadron Leader roaring with laughter once Sgt Wilson had departed.

Squadron Leader: "Sergeant, we must do something to tighten security for access to the main accounts office. Please report back to me A.S.A.P."

Sgt Wilson reports back: "As of tomorrow, airmen will only be able to access EPAS (Equipment Provisioning, Accounting and Supply) using personal identification cards. Photographs will be taken next week and men will receive their cards within three days thereafter."

Squadron Leader: "Get out, you idiot, and bring back to me a list of specific unknown problems we will encounter."

Squadron Leader: "Sgt Wilson, it has come to my notice that SAC Bristow is late on duty most mornings. The other accounts personnel see this happening and see that you have done nothing. This is bad for morale."

Sgt Wilson: "Sir, SAC Bristow suffers nightmares from his tour of duty in Cyprus combating EOKA terrorists. He is on prescribed medication, which sometimes causes him to oversleep. I don't think I can do anything about it."

Squadron Leader: "You don't think, full stop. Come up with a solution and report back to me before lunch."

Sgt Wilson returns, looking pleased with himself. "I think I have resolved the problem with SAC Bristow. We can give him permission to use the back door; that way no one will see him coming in."

Squadron Leader: "I sometimes wonder if you are a smart arse trying to take the piss out of me or whether you are an imbecile who really believes the stupid things he says. Dismissed."

Of course this all happened back in 1960 and probably the humour is now a bit dated. But at the time I thought it very funny. Possibly I was on the same wavelength as the Squadron Leader and perhaps that is why my thorough dislike of him eventually changed to a lifelong friendship.

FIFTEEN
Time To Leave

Inevitably, the time arrived when my tour of duty was at an end. I approached the Squadron Leader to ask when he could release me in order that I could arrange for my flight to the UK via Adelaide.

"Leave it with me, dear boy," was the response.

By now I thought I knew the Squadron Leader well enough to wait until he raised the subject again. I let four weeks drift by before I accepted that I would have to draw on my courage and beard the lion in his den.

"Have you settled upon a date for me to leave, Squadron Leader?" I enquired.

"I haven't done anything about it," said the Squadron Leader. "I assumed you would want to stay on with me. Why not stay until I can get a replacement? You could settle him in and we could both leave together. I am expecting to be posted to HQ Fighter Command at Stanmore Park; possibly I could arrange for you to be posted there so that you are able to stay with me."

"My worst nightmare," was what I thought but did not say. "It would be an honour to continue to serve you, Squadron Leader," I said, "but my tour of duty was ended a month ago and I must return home now."

The Squadron Leader frowned; a scary sight.

"I don't know what is the matter with you, laddie. We have every comfort here. A cheap, well-stocked bar, a camp cinema and a large swimming pool. What is your problem?"

I deliberately refrained from reminding the Squadron Leader that I did not drink, that the cinema showed, almost exclusively, old cowboy films and that the swimming pool was almost always full of drunks playing water polo. Instead I said:

"Yes, Squadron Leader, every pleasure, except the pleasure of my girlfriend, who is 12,000 miles away, and I wish to return home to her."

"Too much time spent on this range, thinking about women. Leave it with me," said the Squadron Leader.

Another month passed by. In desperation I decided to tackle the Squadron Leader again, but with slightly different tactics.

"Squadron Leader, it has been a privilege to serve under you" (I thought, *not literally, thank goodness*). "I do not wish to leave. Further, I am grateful for the way in which you dealt with my commission application. However, the time has come for me to return to England and to allow another fortunate junior officer to gain the benefits of being taught from your vast experience."

The Squadron Leader sighed heavily.

"Do you really feel you have benefitted from my experience?"

"Undoubtedly, Squadron Leader. I equate your knowledge and experience to that of an Air Commodore. No young, junior officer could reasonably expect to have the benefit of being trained by an officer of your seniority."

The Squadron Leader becomes unusually emotional as his friend Gooner leaves for home.

"If I did not know that you are incapable of original thought, I might think you were taking the piss," said the Squadron Leader. "Although it is certainly true that I should have been promoted long ago. However, you assuredly have benefitted from my guidance and I am not displeased with the progress you have made. Realise you have to leave here sometime. Tell Sergeant Wilson to make your arrangements and tell him to keep me informed."

I told Sergeant Wilson what was wanted and, since I shared the Squadron Leader's opinion of him, I repeated the instructions next day.

Departure day arrived at last. As I was about to board the supply plane to Adelaide, I was astonished to see the Squadron Leader drive up. He clambered out of the Jeep and waddled towards me, arms outstretched, with which he proceeded to envelope me in a huge hug.

"Gooner, dear boy, thank you for all your work. Safe journey; I am sure I shall see you again very soon."

Big sigh from me – probably because the breath is being squeezed out of my body.

So I depart at 6am on the long journey home. My flight to London is a night flight by Eagle Airways on a De Havilland Comet 1. It means I have a whole day to see Adelaide for the last time. I cover as much ground as possible.

First stop is the botanical gardens, which remind me so much of an old English country house garden. Black swans glide across the ponds. The elegant wrought iron and glass Palm House, more than a hundred years old, is my landmark to get my bearings. I bypass the zoo and go straight to the Adelaide Oval. I am fortunate; a match is in progress, South Australia versus Victoria. I spend a happy couple of hours there. I enjoy a wonderful steak sandwich, the quality of which I have never experienced before or since. A friendly Aussie points out the Chairman of the Australian Cricket Board, Sir Donald Bradman. I marvel at this diminutive man, perhaps five feet three inches in height, who terrorised all the world's fast bowlers in his heyday. I leave to cross to St Peter's Cathedral, another building which is a hundred years old and part of Australian heritage. It is built in the gothic style and the entrance makes me recall the Notre Dame in Paris. Onwards to the magnificent Montefiore Park with the amphitheatre in the background, and across the Torrens River, sparkling in the sunshine, to the Elder Park, where again I see the black swans. The train station is nearby and so to Adelaide Airport.

First stop is Singapore. There is plenty of time to visit Changi Village to buy silks and other gifts for those in England. Onwards to Bahrain. Here we stop overnight. As I walk along the harbour I feel around me that aura that is unique to the Middle East. The smell of spices in the air, the turgid waters of the Gulf, the beggars in the streets, the thousands of stars blazing in the clear night sky. The last leg of the journey to London should only take about seven hours, but it takes double that time. The Gulf States have banned travel through their air space. We have to climb into Russia and across the Ural Mountains. The views, even through the small DC windows, are breathtaking and spectacular. I see several rivers running into the Caspian Sea and I am exhilarated, not feeling at all the tiredness of the journey.

London at last. I have some leave then report to the HQ Fighter Command at Stanmore Park. Here I am surprised to find that there is nothing for me to do. Temporarily, I am put in charge of salvage stores. However, I am informed that Squadron Leader Folly will be arriving in two or three weeks, at which time I will be allocated to him as his assistant. Some tearing out of hair occurs.

Four weeks pass by and there is no information about the Squadron Leader's arrival. I make further enquiries. I am told that the Squadron Leader will not now be coming to Stanmore Park. His posting has not been approved by the Air Vice Marshal, who is Commanding Officer at Stanmore Park. That evening I take my girlfriend to the Pigalle nightclub to celebrate.

I am left kicking my heels for the next few months as my term of duty comes to an end. I am still in charge of salvage stores, but there is little work to do and I am happy enough to spend time on extra training, as I am still boxing at senior level.

My term of duty is now ended. I am offered a further term of seven years. I ask if my rank can be made substantive and paid. I am told not at present, but if I sign on for a further term my position will be reviewed in six months' time. I felt this was grossly unfair and, for some strange reason, I imagined that the Squadron Leader had something to do with the decision. I left the RAF for pastures new.

SIXTEEN
Home

I am back in civvy street. No more free accommodation, food, clothing and spending money. I actually have to work to survive. The RAF had given me 32 weeks of training as an accountant and I had taken a correspondence course; I was now a qualified accountant. This was the only work I could get that would pay me enough to live on.

After a couple of short-term jobs, I found myself employed as accountant to a publishing company in Edgware Road, London. The owner was an arrogant, pompous would-be MP who, some 50 plus years on, is now a Tory grandee peer. I detested him and always left the office for at least an hour at lunchtime to get away from him.

A new casino had opened near to the office and offered free sandwiches and coffee at lunchtime. For some weeks this was my midday haven at no cost. Eventually the freebies came to an end. I decided to walk down to the Victory Club at Marble Arch. Here, serving and ex-RAF personnel could get hot food and drinks at a subsidized cost. I was nicely settled with "Victory Hotpot" and a large coffee when a booming voice rang out.

"Gooner, old chap, what the devil are you doing here?"

A heavy clap on the shoulder knocked me sideways and sent the hotpot spinning.

"Sorry about that, Gooner. Let me get you another," said the Squadron Leader. Moving amazingly quickly for a man of his huge size, the Squadron Leader was soon back with two bowls of the steaming mixture. His face beaming with delight, he demanded full details of my life since Maralinga.

"How is that girlfriend you were so keen to get back home to?"

"I gave her up. Nothing seemed the same after 20 months under your command, Squadron Leader."

"Haw, haw. Made a man out of you. Got something a bit more raunchy now, have you? Haw, haw."

I decided to change the subject.

"What are you doing at the Victory Club, sir?"

"Live here, old boy. Got a nice little bachelor flat on the third floor. Fully serviced." The Squadron Leader then launched into a tirade against the RAF medical officers who had terminated his service due to 'poor physical condition'. "Disgraceful," he said, "not a man in the RAF fitter than me. You know that, Gooner."

At that moment a voice behind me said "Good afternoon, sir," and I turned to see Jock Mulcahy clicking his heels and throwing an extravagant salute.

"That is my manservant, haw, haw!" roared the Squadron Leader.

I exchanged telephone numbers with the Squadron Leader and Jock and later that day I phoned Jock.

"Are you working for the Squadron Leader now?"

"Yes, I am still his batman. I am living with my sister nearby, so it's convenient."

"Surely you had enough of him in Maralinga? Couldn't you get a better job than that?

"No, sir, I couldn't. Had a bit of trouble with the law before I joined the RAF."

"What do you do for him now, Jock?"

"Same as before. Attend him first thing in the morning and last thing at night. Make sure he has clean, pressed clothes. Ensure supplies of Johnnie Black are always in stock."

"Jock, please keep an eye on him to make sure he is not permanently pissed."

"Will do, sir."

I was not left with many days to ruminate on events before the Squadron Leader telephoned to invite me to dinner. I went along to the Victory Club, anticipating more hotpot and tales of the Squadron Leader. To my surprise, the Squadron Leader said:

"We are going to a nice little bistro in Notting Hill, where they look after me very well."

We walked round the corner in to Seymour Street, where Jock was waiting in an elderly Rover.

"Is this yours?" I asked the Squadron Leader.

"Yes, left to me by a fellow resident at the Club."

"But where do you park?" I asked.

"Victory Club deliveries car park," laughed the Squadron Leader.

It was a short drive to Notting Hill and here the Squadron Leader told Jock to return in two hours. It was a magnificent meal. Veal escalope in a mouth-watering light batter, with spaghetti pomodoro. Tiramisu to die for. Complimented by a Pouilly Fuisse wine and finished with a Hennessy brandy for me and a very large Johnnie Black for himself. I can still taste all the wonderful flavours as though it were only yesterday. In the course of the meal I learned that the Squadron Leader had remained at Maralinga a further six months, during which my successor had, in the Squadron Leader's own words, "driven me to distraction with his ineptitude". Returning home, the Squadron Leader had been posted to RAF Lyneham, HQ Transport Command. The Station C.O. had insisted on his having a full medical, which had resulted in his retirement. He was still raving about "medical maniacs" when Jock arrived to return us to base.

On the way back, the Squadron Leader confided to me that, although he was very contented at the Victory Club, he did feel the need of finding a good woman to share his life. After such a splendid meal I felt it would be churlish of me to point out that his physical appearance would be a great deterrent to such a quest. Instead I advised him to try a good marriage bureau.

SEVENTEEN
The Squadron Leader Meets A Lady

Following that enjoyable evening, I received several telephone calls from the Squadron Leader over a period of five or six weeks. Always in good humour, talking about new interests in his life and cracking jokes in his inimitable fashion. So I was not surprised when I got a call from him inviting me to dinner at the Dorchester Hotel in Park Lane. But I was surprised when he informed me that his other guests were "Margaret, a most charming Scottish lady I met through a marriage agency, and her best friend Jean". I duly met the party in the main bar and was introduced to Margaret, who matched the Squadron Leader in size and age and was not much better looking. Her friend, Jean, was what is termed "a bonnie Scots lassie", in her late thirties and, I thought, quite sexy. The Squadron Leader explained that this was to be a small engagement party, "Margaret having consented to be my lady wife".

At this the two ladies smiled broadly and excused themselves for a visit to the powder room. The Squadron Leader is in high humour.

"I've landed a good one here, Gooner, old chap. Filthy rich and a large estate outside Dalkeith, quite close to Edinburgh. Plenty of hunting, fishing and good Scotch whisky. Ha ha. She insisted on bringing a best friend along tonight and upon me bringing my best friend to make four. Hope you don't mind, dear boy. You'll be best man at the wedding, of course." I am unsure of my feelings about my new status.

"When is the wedding?" I enquire.

"Very soon. Registry office. Honeymoon will be at her estate. Time I had a good woman to support me. You said so yourself."

I do not recall this, but I let it pass. The ladies return and an excellent meal follows. I note that Margaret keeps pace with the Squadron Leader in the drinking bout that ensues. Jean and I are also drinking heavily. The Squadron Leader announces that we will all stay at the Dorchester overnight, and sends me off to book rooms. I book two double rooms. Jean does not protest.

The wedding takes place at Caxton Hall in Westminster and there are no problems. There is a small reception in The Directors Club nearby. I attend with Jean; Jock with his sister are there and the party is made up with a tall, impressive looking fellow whom the Squadron Leader refers to as "Flashy" and he is accompanied by a woman I can only euphemistically describe as an "escort". I later learn that the man's name is Flashman and that he claims to be a relative of the distinguished war hero from the Victorian era, General Sir Harry Flashman, V. C. The Squadron Leader and Margaret consume huge quantities of champagne. The Squadron Leader instructs Jock to inform the Victory Club that he is on a long vacation and asked him to keep an eye on the flat. The happy (?) couple depart. The Squadron Leader announces that he has no idea when they will be back.

EIGHTEEN
Gooner To The Rescue

It is several weeks before I hear from the Squadron Leader again. There is panic, almost terror in his voice.

"Gooner, you must come up to Scotland at once."

"Why must I come up to Scotland at once, Squadron Leader? I am working as accountant to Michael Heseltine and he is a very demanding man."

"So am I. It is a matter of urgency. Margaret is dead. I am being blackmailed by the ghillie and screwed by the Procurator Fiscal."

"You are in bed with the Procurator Fiscal? I don't understand."

"No, no. The Procurator is trying to screw me financially. You are the only one who can get me out of this. You are the only one I know who is on the same wavelength as thieves and blackmailers."

"Thanks for the compliment. Seems like you have got even your enormous knickers in a twist. OK, I can come within a few days."

Arriving at Dalkeith, I ask the ancient taxi driver for the Cameron Estate.

"Not going there, mate. Procurator Fiscal is dancing about up there."

He directs me to a pony and cart. When I get there, the Squadron Leader is already pacing up and down the driveway.

"We won't go into the House. Ghillie's there. Come over to the pagoda."

"What's all the panic about?" I ask.

"Things had not been going well with Margaret. She didn't understand I am the boss. Lots of bad feeling. Sex no good. Suggested a day out hunting and a picnic. Went with ghillie in pony and cart. Stopped at Kings Cross. Margaret stumbles as she gets out of cart; shotgun goes off and blows her brains out. I am shocked, but you know something like that can't upset a Battle of Britain pilot for long. I think that things have not been going well but I am now Laird of the Manor. I tell the ghillie to drive back to the house and be quick about it. I call 'the polis' and the local doctor and go in search of my case of Johnnie Walker Black Label, which Margaret has hidden. There didn't seem to be a problem, although the polis questioned the ghillie for some time. He looked very sour-faced and was in bad humour for the rest of the day. After the funeral the polis said they wanted to take me to the office of the Procurator Fiscal. The Procurator asked if I had found any will; I said not. The Procurator then produced a will in which Margaret had left her estate to Scottish Heritage. Nothing for me and, as we had been married less than 12 months, I have no claim under Scottish law. To make matters worse, the ghillie is blackmailing me."

I ask: "How blackmailing you?"

The Squadron Leader tells me: "He wants redundancy money and if he doesn't get it, he will remember I was the last one to hold the gun. You have to help me."

"You must get a solicitor," I said.

"I can't afford one," sighed the Squadron Leader. "The expense of that woman has near bankrupted me. If anyone knows how to deal with these cunning Scots it is you, Goony."

My heart sank as I heard that over-familiar form of address. There was much to think about. I was tempted to pour a large "Johnnie" for myself. I resisted and sat down quietly and called for tea, which the ghillie served, accompanied by a supercilious look on his weather-beaten face.

Tea can be an inspirational drink in the appropriate circumstances. I would deal with the ghillie first. I put it to the ghillie that if he accused the Squadron Leader, and it was then found his fingerprints were not on the shotgun, then the ghillie would be charged with perverting the course of justice. The ghillie's smile was almost as horrible as the Squadron Leader's.

"His prints will be on the gun awright," he guffawed.

Time to change tactics. "What do you want?" I asked.

"Ah've lorst me job. I need £5,000," he moaned.

The door had opened and I leapt in.

"The Squadron Leader will ensure that you are kept on here as caretaker and will give you £1,000 as a bonus for your long service. Alternatively I will inform the Procurator that I overheard you blackmailing the Squadron Leader."

"Ye heid nay sich thing, ye Sassenach swine," roared the ghillie.

"Final offer," I said.

The ghillie stroked his beard awhile, then stretched out his hand. "Done."

Now to deal with the Procurator Fiscal. His offices, in Edinburgh, were splendid Victoriana with magnificent gardens. He sat behind a huge desk on a throne-like chair at one end of an enormous room. He too was enormous. I gave him my No.1 smile and said:

"Very good of you to spare me a few moments, Procurator. I won't delay you. I think I can quickly settle the matter of the Lady Margaret's estate with you."

"Nothing to settle," growled the Procurator, "the estate is ours."

"That is for the English courts to decide," I answered him. "The Squadron Leader is a lawfully wedded husband and he is English and will be heard in an English court, unless we can compromise."

"What compromise?" demanded the Procurator.

"The Squadron Leader would like to return to London and take with him his wife's personal jewellery and would not pursue the matter further."

"The jewellery is worth many thousands," said the Procurator.

"Sentimental reasons," said I.

"Done," said the Procurator.

"There is one more thing. The ghillie would like to stay on."

The Procurator stroked his beard. "Well, someone has got to look after the place and I have no time to be looking around for a caretaker. Ghillie knows the land. Done."

I rose to leave. The Procurator did not shake my hand.

I reported back to the Squadron Leader. Once he had grasped the fact that he had no rights to the estate, he was more than satisfied to be able to leave with thousands of pounds' worth of jewellery and no threat from the ghillie.

"I am overjoyed, my boy," he shouted. "I must get out of this miserable, freezing country immediately." So saying, he lunged at me with the clear intention of kissing me. Fortunately, in those days, I was nimble enough to avoid 30 stone of blubber.

By the following afternoon we were back in London and I left him in Victory House, nursing his old friend, Johnnie Walker Black Label. I said a silent prayer that there would be a long period of relief before I was called again to deal with the Squadron Leader's problems.

NINETEEN
The Squadron Leader Is Set Upon

My prayers were answered. It was many weeks before I was again drawn into the Squadron Leader's chaotic world. When the call came it was in the middle of the night and it was not a pleasant one.

It is 2am. I am asleep. The telephone is ringing persistently. I fumble for it. A voice announces itself as Sergeant Ryder from Edgware Road police.

"We have Squadron Leader Folly here. We are unable to contact his man Jock and yours is the only other number we have. We do not want to keep him here and are prepared to release him into your custody."

I explained that I was in North London and it was not convenient; they would have to keep him until the morning.

"Well," said Sergeant Ryder, "we will just lock him in the cells and in the morning we will charge him with being drunk and exposing himself in public."

I insisted on knowing how the Squadron Leader came to be arrested.

"We found him drunk and naked outside the Old Kings Head at the Marylebone end of Edgware Road."

Under these circumstances I felt I had to go and rescue the old boy.

There was no problem in getting him released without charge. When I got him back to Victory House I demanded to know how the police came to find him in that condition.

"Well," said the Squadron Leader, "Jock took me to the Old Kings Head for a birthday drink. Two ex-RAF Lyneham chaps recognised Jock and, on learning it was my birthday, bought a round of doubles. I returned the compliment and Jock weighed in. I remember some tarty woman joined us and I remember nothing more until the police woke me up outside the pub. Everything was gone: clothes, wallet, watch, the lot. I was set up and robbed."

Experience had taught me to have little sympathy with the old drunk, but this occasion was an exception. I settled him down and left, telling him I wanted no more middle of the night phone calls.

In fact it was many weeks before I heard from him again. I was bidden to lunch at the Reform Club to hear "news of life-changing importance". This so intrigued me, thoughts of transgender buzzing through my head, that I accepted immediately. My first question on arrival was:

"How did you get in here? You surely are not a member?"

Huge distorted wink. "Secretary served under me at Northolt and, yes, he did survive."

Paté, steak and kidney pudding and apple pie were consumed before the Squadron Leader told me what was on his mind.

"I am leaving this wet, miserable country. It is full of moral turpitude. I am going back to Australia and there I shall stay."

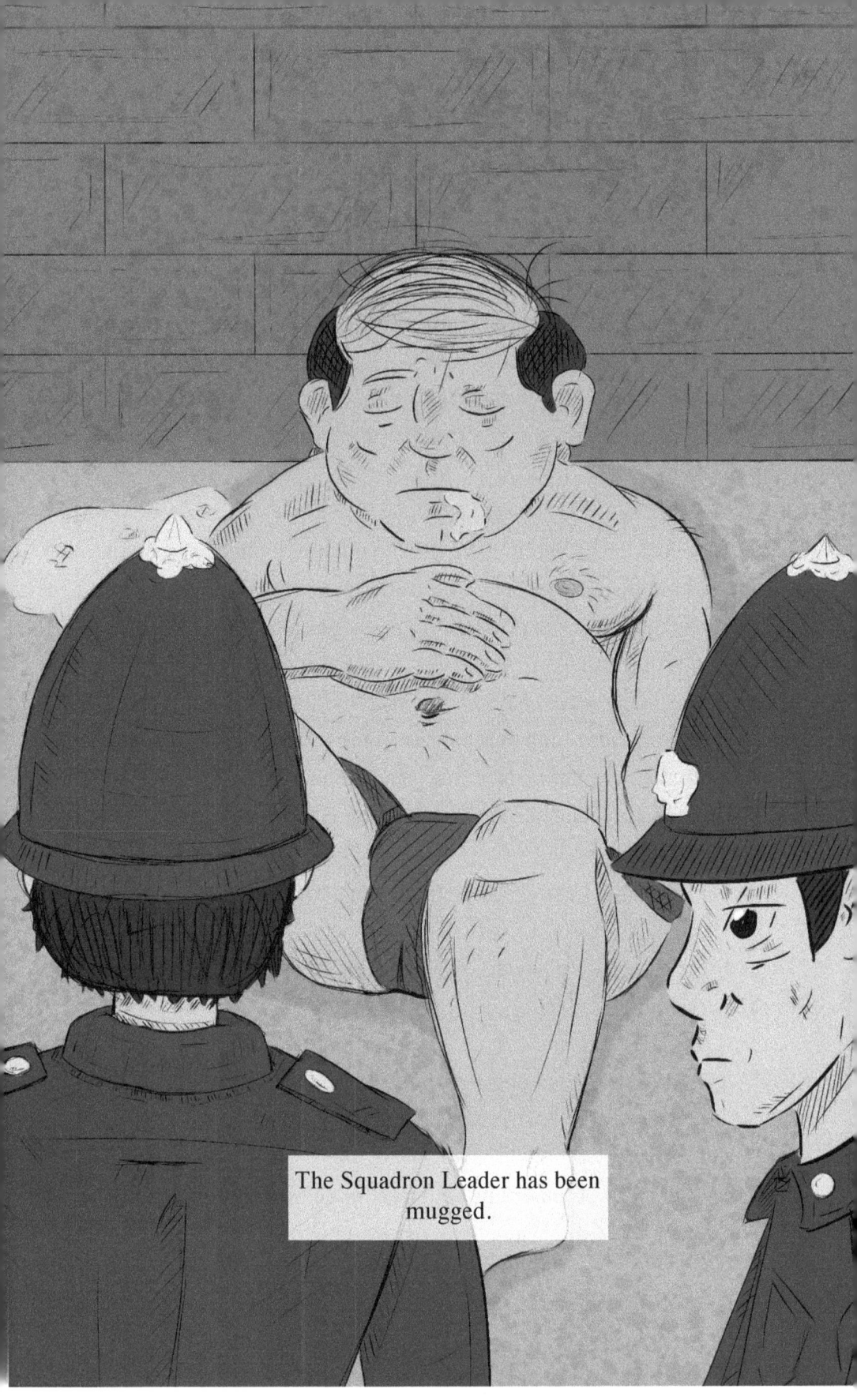

The Squadron Leader has been mugged.

TWENTY
Nostalgia

"What's with the moral turpitude thing?" I asked. "Is it about what happened to you at the Old Kings Head?"

"Not really. It is the general deterioration in the way people behave. It isn't the world I grew up in. Manners just are not the same. No concept of praise or of blame. I shan't be sorry to leave."

"Where will you stay?"

"Initially at Watson. No trains running past there anymore. Old Robbo has bought the Station premises. He says there is loads of room and I can stay as long as I like."

"It's very isolated and Robbo has always been a bit of a hermit," I said. "You will be terribly lonely."

"I have a nostalgia for the old place and anyway I am fed up with people. If I am on my own I will have someone sensible to have a conversation with."

There really was no answer to that so I bade him "bon voyage" and left him to his large Johnnie Walker and the bill.

The Squadron Leader decided it would be inappropriate not to give a leaving party before giving Australia the pleasure of his company. I was told I was to be "the special guest". No way of refusing then.

I was surprised to find nearly 20 people turned up. I wouldn't have thought the old bugger had that many friends who would make a journey to see him. Although the thought of getting rid of him may well have been an incentive.

My old boxing chum, Dick McTaggert, turned up. We had boxed in the same RAF team together and I had not seen him since for some years and made no apology for monopolising his time. It seems he knew the Squadron Leader from his time in Scotland.

Also there was a quite attractive F.O. who had come down from Ashington to see him off. They were very close all evening but no one seemed to know what the relationship was. I fancied her myself but, knowing the strength of the Squadron Leader's vile temper, I deemed it best not to interfere. As the party began to break up, someone asked the Squadron Leader if he remembered an incident he was involved in at Famagusta, Cyprus, in which a fire was started which caused the officers' mess bar to close. The Squadron Leader replied with one of his trademark jokes. "Only vaguely. Memory not what it was. Went to see my private doctor last month. I told him I am getting really forgetful. I forget where I have parked my car. I go into shops and can't remember what I want, and when I do get to the checkout, I find I have forgotten my wallet. It is getting worse. What can I do, doctor? Doctor said, 'pay me in advance'."

At this point I made my exit.

After a delay of many weeks due to Australian immigration issues, the Squadron Leader finally departed and I thought that would be the last I would hear of him for a very long time. My hopes were not to be realised. The first of a barrage of phone calls came less than a month after his departure.

"Gooner. I have settled in at Watson with Robbo. Been up to Maralinga. It is just a ghost area. All the admin buildings are gone. The airstrip remains but is overgrown. I went to the forward area, no one and nothing there. But it is still guarded. Rails and posts and a little hut. Two very scruffy RAAF airmen with dirty, open neck shirts. I told them who I am and that I had come from the UK to have a look around for old times' sake. The one says 'I don't care who you are. No one allowed on site.' The other one says 'I have heard of you. Give us a drop of whisky' and starts loud, cackling laughter. I told him if he had been one of my men he would have been on a charge. They start throwing stones at me so I leave. Won't go back, Goony.

"I have encountered a problem with Johnnie. I picked up six bottles from duty-free on the way out, just for emergencies. When I got here, I found Robbo drinks only canned beer and won't touch spirits. He knows what I drink and he never mentioned a word. Spiteful bugger. But why be spiteful when he has invited me to stay? The nearest place I can get supplies is Coorable, which is about 200 miles away. Robbo refused to lend me the Jeep. More spite. I had to wait four days until a hobo friend of his turned up with food supplies and I had to bribe the bugger heavily to drive me to Coorable. Bought an old banger in Coora and drove myself back. Storeman only had half a dozen Johnnie, so took his few bottles of Teachers and Famous Grouse in desperation. Asked him to order six cases of Johnnie, offering to pay in advance, but he would not do it. Still have an account with JW, but they will only dispatch overseas if the order is made in the UK and paid in advance. Could you help out? Please phone JW, say you are me, my account number is FOL 0705, and ask them to send six cases of Black Label in my name to Coorable Station, South Australia. Victory House are holding a large deposit on my behalf and I have telexed them to release £1,000 to you which should be enough to cover advance payment to JW. Matter of urgency, Goony old chap. I am already getting withdrawal symptoms."

This was followed by daily phone calls, each one more incoherent than the previous, until the supplies actually arrived.

Their arrival did not stop the phone calls.

The time came, inevitably, as I knew it would, when the Squadron Leader phoned to tell me he was moving on from Watson.

"I have had a big row with Robbo and he has told me to go."

I asked, "What was the row about?"

"It has been building up for a while. I had a drop too much Johnnie one night, lost my balance and knocked over a chair. Robbo fell over it and injured his leg. He showed me the leg and told me it hurts. Asked me what he should do. I said 'limp'. He accused me of making sarcastic remarks and said it was the lowest form of wit.

"Also he has been cooking a lot of rotten food, which has been making my stomach do the Hallelujah Chorus."

I interrupted, "That's a lot of stomach to heave."

"Yaas," says the Squadron Leader. "Well, one night when I was telling him about my experiences on the Rocket Range and explaining what a shower of shit my airmen were, he suddenly says 'you're boring the arse off me' and lets out a noisy fart. Well, I thought that was downright ignorant, so I let out one of my 'specials', which was certainly very ripe, having had the benefit of his lousy grub and a few drams of Johnnie.

"'You vile creature,' he shouts. 'You constantly stink the place out. You must find somewhere else to live.' I rushed at him and he let out another fart and fled in terror. So I will have to go. I will go down to Adelaide next week. Any suggestions?"

"The Queens is still the only good hotel in Adelaide. The Barman now has permanent stocks of Johnnie Walker Black. Gladys is still there and still attractive. She will look after you very well."

"Goony, don't know what I would do without you. Even from 12,500 miles away."

Silently I am saying, "May it stay that way". Yet, curiously, a few moments later I am regretting the thought.

It must have been a month or more before I heard from the old bugger again.

"Gooner, I am well settled in at The Queens and you were right about Gladys. She is again looking after me very well. As you say, she is mature and I do like them young and nubile. But she is a real goer and I am in attendance, know what I mean, nudge, nudge. But I am already getting tired of Adelaide; it is a bit of a one horse town. I am thinking of moving on to Melbourne and the good thing is, Gladys says she will come with me."

There was little I could say to that other than "keep me posted".

I do not hear anything for some months. I then receive a very long and garrulous call in which the Squadron Leader tells me he has settled in Melbourne and gives me his views, at length, on that city.

"I am settled in Melbourne and Gladys is with me. It has changed an awful lot and is much busier than Adelaide. There are no restrictions on building heights. The I.C.I. building has been completed and skyscrapers are going up everywhere. New indoor shopping malls, American style, are being built. Fancy shops have taken the place of the old mansions on St Kilda Road. The noise and dust from building works is appalling. I have a large apartment down by the harbour. Gladys will not live with me, but has found a job in a café on Hoddle Street, with a little flat above. Stand by for an announcement soon."

The next communication was a letter, telling me he had proposed to Gladys.

"She has told me to ask her again when I have lost ten stone and have cut down on Johnnie. What she doesn't know about Johnnie won't hurt her, but I am going to have a go at the weight loss thing. Will keep you posted."

In fact, some weeks passed with no word, so I decided to phone him.

"What is the news?" I enquire. "How is the weight?"

"Nothing wrong with the weight. But I have had a big setback. Paid a surprise visit to Gladys at the coffee shop and found her in close contact with a very well dressed but lecherous looking cove. 'Who is this?' I demanded. Gladys says, 'This is my friend Rupert.' He says, 'And who are you?' I roar at him. 'I am Squadron Leader Folly.' 'Squadron Leader Balloon more like,' he says. So I walk my 30 stone into him and he crashes into a chair, breaking it. Gladys calls me a hooligan and tells me to get out before she loses her job. It is some days before she will speak to me and when we meet she says our relationship is over. She says the sex is no good because I am so overweight and she always has to be on top and that Johnnie stinks and I reek of it. Well, I didn't resist. The insult to Johnnie went too far. J. W. Black has a beautiful bouquet and has been my friend for a very long time. Naturally I am feeling a bit low."

I had known the Squadron Leader too long not to be sympathetic.

"Cheer up," I said. "You don't want to get too involved at your age. I haven't been in Melbourne since I left you in Maralinga, but there were plenty of loose women there then and I am sure there still are. Have fun."

Major changes are happening in my life and I do not have time to think about the Squadron Leader.

Quite unexpectedly I receive a message to contact him urgently. I phone and my first words are:

"How are you getting on? Have you found a lady to your taste?"

"No, I have not. You were certainly right in saying there are plenty of loose women around. One of them has given me the clap."

I said, "Hurrah."

"I didn't say clap, you fool, I said I've got the clap. I blame it on you, Gooner. As soon as I have got rid of this disease I am returning home. You had better get round to Victory House and make sure my old donga is available."

I go to see the Accommodation Officer at Victory House. When I tell him the Squadron Leader is returning, he throws up his hands in horror.

"There is no accommodation for him here. We are completely full and have a waiting list. We would not have him anyway. When he was here he bored everybody to death with his tales of forbearance in Maralinga."

I phone the Squadron Leader to tell him there is no accommodation available at Victory House. He lets out a long, weary sigh like an old horse farting.

"You would think they would keep quarters available for an old, wounded war hero. No matter. Jock's niece is vacating her flat in Seymour Place. Getting married to a Squadron Leader, would you believe. Lucky cow. The landlord is reserving it for me on Jock's recommendation."

I went ballistic. "What the hell did you get me running around to Victory House for then?"

"Had to find out whether they would let me down. And if you are going to adopt that tone of voice with me, you can address me as Sir."

I slam the phone down. I never cease to wonder at the Squadron Leader's line of thought.

TWENTY-ONE
The Squadron Leader Returns

Several weeks pass before I hear the joyous (?) news that the Squadron Leader is fit again and on the way back.

"Got a scheduled flight with Eagle Airways on one of the new De Havilland Comets. Better than the Hercules Transport Aircraft, what! I shall be stopping off in Singapore for a few days, staying at the Britannia. Can't stay at Raffles; they have had a big fire. Most inconvenient."

The next communication informs me to collect him at Heathrow. I wonder if I am still in the RAF. He arrives full of fun. First stop is the duty-free shop to load up with Black Label. Then on to Seymour Place, where Jock is waiting for us and throws the Squadron Leader a huge salute.

"At ease, Aircraftsman, and get that Johnnie open. Let's all have a large dram."

I remind the Squadron Leader that I do not drink whisky. I do not tell him that I am now working as accountant to a firm of whisky blenders where I have available a large staff discount.

The Squadron Leader decides to host a small dinner party as a house-warming and to celebrate his homecoming. Jock's niece, Julie, and her fiancé are invited, but he declines. He knows the Squadron Leader by reputation amongst his peers.

"Full of sarcastic jokes. Not my type at all," he tells Julie.

The Squadron Leader calls at my flat to tell me Julie is not coming.

"A great pity," he says. "She is such a pretty girl. Could you get a couple of good looking women to join us, Goony?"

"I am not a pimp, you know, Squadron Leader."

"No, no. Of course not, Goony. I would find two swingers myself if I weren't so busy arranging the dinner."

The thought of the Squadron Leader's two swingers persuaded me to do a U-turn.

"OK. Leave it with me. I will see what I can do."

"I know I can rely on you, Goony, wink, wink, nudge, nudge."

I asked my girlfriend, Jean, if she would like to come. She said she would, but there was a problem as she had promised to visit her lonely mother, Phyllis, that night.

"Would she like to come, do you think?"

Jean said she was sure she would and so it was arranged. Jean's mother was an attractive 45-year-old with a good sense of humour. Problem solved.

We were six for dinner. My three, the Squadron Leader and Jock, with a boyfriend. We were served by a gorgeous, big-titted, red-headed young "lady" whom the Squadron Leader described as a friend. The Squadron

Leader was in good form, regaling us with a series of inoffensive jokes and anecdotes, including one of his favourites about being in a pub when a fellow officer offered him £20 if he could drink 12 large whiskies in 12 minutes. The Squadron Leader told him to line them up whilst he excused himself for a moment and left the pub. Returning in a few minutes he promptly demolished the dozen whiskies. Asked where he had been, he said he had been to the pub next door to make sure he could do it.

The evening went very well and, when liqueurs were served, the Squadron Leader beckoned me out onto the balcony.

"Goony, you have done it again, old chap. Phyllis is a cracker and a real goer, unless I am much mistaken. I am taking her to dinner at The Dorchester next week. I will book a room and if I can't get her to commit some indiscretion, my name's not Folly, ha, ha, ha."

I said, "Be careful, Squadron Leader, remember your Melbourne experience."

The Squadron Leader turned very frosty at that and shortly afterwards announced that the evening was over. When we left the Squadron Leader said his friend would stay to help him clean up. At this, Jock's boyfriend started giggling and had to be quietened by a very black look from Jock. Thus the evening ended.

Over the course of the next few weeks the Squadron Leader was in constant contact with me, mostly by telephone, but also heaving himself out to my flat in Snaresbrook to talk to me in person. Since his return he had been at somewhat of a loss to know what to do with his time. When he had been at the Victory Club, there had always been a captive audience to listen to his stories and activities in which to participate. Now he was no longer welcome there. My line was that there were plenty of other clubs in London and he might find somewhere like The Reform Club or The Garrick to his liking, where gentlemen gathered in the afternoons to drink, lunch, chat, read papers. I knew two or three acquaintances who might put his name forward. He thought it an excellent idea.

His name was put forward at The Reform Club and duly considered by the committee. He came to see me at Snaresbrook and I could tell immediately from his filthy temper that they had rejected him.

"No reason given," he raged. "If they don't want a man of my status they must be a bunch of ignorant old farts. Not the types I wish to favour with my presence. I am going to see the Secretary at The Garrick next week. Will keep you posted. I have brought a bottle of Johnnie with me, but I know it is not your tipple, so I have brought you a bottle of Pouilly-Fuissé."

Before I could say I was not drinking, a large glass of each had been poured. Before I was halfway through my glass was topped up and the Squadron Leader was finishing his third glass. He then settled himself into my best armchair and began to snore like a warthog. I decided to give up, leave him there and go to bed. I must say the wine relaxed me and I slept well. When I awoke, the Squadron Leader had gone, but his aroma remained to remind me of his presence.

Eager for news of his Garrick interview, it was I who phoned the Squadron Leader on this occasion.

"I've met with Bobby, the Secretary; a very decent sort. Takes a dram of Johnnie, would you believe. He is putting my name forward himself so I am sure of acceptance. Entry and subscription fees are pretty stiff, but I think it is a good option. As you say, I can go any day and have a yarn and a doss around."

I left it about a month before I enquired further. "Things going alright at The Garrick?"

A long pause, then the Squadron Leader says, "I did join and I go there most days. There is no shortage of actors to drink with, but most of them are gay, not really my type. I have met an agent who says he can get me work as a character actor; says my looks are most unusual. But he wants me to take an expensive acting course and wants to charge 30% of any fees I get for work, so I think I will swerve him."

I told him I thought he had always had great character and been a bit of an actor without benefit of drama lessons and that he should keep an open mind. I didn't tell him my private hope that getting involved with an agent might lead to me having to listen to less of his moaning.

I was pleased to think he had settled in at the Garrick and hoped it would be a long-time occupation for his time. I should have known better. He was soon phoning me to tell me he had quit The Garrick.

"Had two or three bad experiences lending money to chaps. Bad idea. They are all skint and full of overweening ambition. Never did like those poncey actors much anyway."

"What is your next move?" I enquired.

"I met some horsey types at The Reform who have asked me to undertake some discreet, confidential commissions for them. They are entertaining me at Sandown Park racecourse next week to outline what they want and what they have to offer. As always, I will keep you posted."

TWENTY-TWO
The Squadron Leader Goes Racing

Being a racing man myself I was most interested in what the Squadron Leader was up to with his new contacts. Hearing nothing for four weeks, I took the bull by the horns (literally!) and phoned him.

"Been very busy, old chap. Very exciting. These people are a syndicate who pay for information on when horses are expected to win or lose. They are well known to bookmakers so cannot get large bets on. They rely on a selected few individuals like myself to get wagers on for them. They usually bet to win but they have some clever variations. For example, if they get information that a fancied horse in a big race next week will not run, then they lay it to lose. Being an ante post bet, if the horse does not run, it is a loser; thus they win. One thing I don't like is that I have to send their winnings, less my commission, in cash to what is obviously a council flat in the East End of London."

I told the Squadron Leader it sounded illegal to me and warned him not to place any bets with his own money. He said they were always in credit with him and that if it was suspicious in any way then they would not dare to withhold any money owed to him.

I said, "You know best, Squadron Leader."

As the reader might suspect, it was not many weeks before I received a call from the Squadron Leader, unloading his grievances on me.

"Those racing syndicate bastards owe me three grand that I can't recover."

I said, "I told you not to bet with your own money. What happened?"

"Last week they had a couple of losers so were no longer in credit. Then, ten minutes before a race was due to start, they asked me to place a bet. I said the arrangement was I don't bet with my money, but they said there was no time to get the money to my bank and swore upon their honour as gentlemen that, if they lost, the money would be in my bank the next day. They lost. The money was not put in to my bank and I heard no further from them. I telephoned several times without answer, until finally an operator told me the line was no longer in existence. Then I got hold of one of my old Sergeants, not that idiot Wilson, this one is working in the security industry. I gave him a letter of authority and asked him to go to their flat and try to get my money. He attended but confirmed it is a council flat, now deserted and boarded up. I've been done. Their word of honour is as a piss in the wind when compared to their greed."

I asked, "How does your loss compare with the commissions you deducted?"

"I broke about even. That is not the point. I spent a lot of time over several weeks, I've been let down and, on top of that, my bank manager is asking why I've been gambling thousands of pounds, says it affects any reference the bank might be asked to give. Might have known I would get little sympathy from you. You don't understand these things."

"Then why ask my advice in the first place?"

"I can listen to advice but I don't have to take it."

"You should know after all these years, Squadron Leader, that I always give sound advice."

"Humbug."

End of conversation.

TWENTY-THREE
The Squadron Leader Starts His Own Company

I decided to leave the Squadron Leader to nurse his ill humour alone and did not contact him for some weeks.

I began to hear from ex-comrades that he seemed to be at a loose end, not knowing what to do with his time. He had taken up, and given up, scuba diving. He had joined a snooker club where he had been fleeced of a good deal of money. I was told he had lunched several times with a stockbroker in Threadneedle Street with a view to making investments in the stock market. I heard from Jock that he was getting up later and later in the day, not knowing what to do with himself.

Time to make contact.

I asked how he was and what he had been doing with himself.

"I've been at a bit of a loss to know what to do with my time. But I am glad you rang. I've found a new venture to fully occupy me and your involvement is essential. Also I want you to meet one of my old Sergeants, Drysdale. I will give one of my famous lunches next week and all will be revealed."

The lunch was at Bistro La Boite at Notting Hill. A quiet restaurant, laid out in booths. Sadly no longer there. Sergeant Nigel Drysdale was a small, dapper man with a toothbrush moustache. The Squadron Leader wasted no time but went straight into an introduction. Sergeant Drysdale had served under the Squadron Leader at Northolt. He was now working as a trainer for a small security company. He had told the Squadron Leader that there was a high demand for security services within the Home Counties, mainly due to the police no longer having the capacity to deal with burglaries and vandalism. The Sergeant had suggested that the Squadron Leader would find it very interesting to form his own security company. The Squadron Leader said that, before he could consider entering into such a venture, he would need assurances of help from those he could trust, such as former colleagues. Sergeant Drysdale had already said he would leave his present job and would be happy to work under the Squadron Leader again. He could bring with him a substantial contract requiring two guards night and day. He was also in contact with Corporal Lump, ex-RAF Regiment, who had served with them at Northolt. He would make an excellent Inspector. At this point, the Sergeant asked to be excused, as he was due back on duty.

As soon as he had left the Squadron Leader became very animated.

"I am going to do this. I need an interest and I need to see some money coming in. I am happy to employ Drysdale but that is as far as I go with him. That is where you come in, Goony, old chap."

I was on instant alert. Here we go again; he is going to dump some problem on me.

"I want you to take this project on. What I want you to do is register a limited company and find some suitable premises. I have identified Kingston upon Thames as a rapidly expanding town. Lots of office blocks, shops and supermarkets being built, many building sites. Everywhere needing security."

This did not seem too onerous so I said I would try to deal with it.

"Goony, when you first came to me, age 20, I identified you as a Mr Fixit, that is why I made sure you were commissioned. I know you can sort anything. Go to it, my boy."

He then rose, threw money on the table and walked out. Despite the many years I had known him, the Squadron Leader's behaviour still occasionally amazed me.

Being Mr Fixit does not mean doing everything yourself. It does mean knowing a man who can. One phone call to Michael, Douglas & Co, a company specialising in registrations, and the Squadron Leader had his company. Finding premises was not too difficult either. The Squadron Leader had identified Kingston upon Thames and I already knew one of the partners at the main commercial surveyors, Bonsor Pennington. He soon found me a floor in an old office block on the London Road. It readily divided into three offices: Management, General Office and a twenty-four-hour Control Room. A separate room in an adjoining annexe was ideal as a training room. Lease terms were exceptionally generous.

I was soon able to report back to the Squadron Leader.

He positively bounced with enthusiasm.

"Goony, I want you to take this project over and run it."

"I already have a job, Sir."

"Quit it. This is not a job. You will be Managing Director. You will have a 20% shareholding. You will draw a salary of £25,000 per annum, plus your dividends and a company car."

I asked, "How would you want me to set about it?"

The Squadron Leader growled with laughter. "You probably know better than I do. Prepare a five year budget. Bottom line is £30,000 net profit year one, moving through the gears to £100,000 net profit year five. I will put £50,000 capital in. Go to the Royal Bank in Kingston for a £50,000 start-up loan. I will guarantee. Hire all staff yourself. Drysdale will train them to British Securities Industry standard. They will draw their uniforms from Chalmers & Co at Wandsworth, a firm owned by one of my ex-fellow officers. Corporal Lump will then take them over. You will deal with all accounting and financial matters, human resources and management of sites. I will act as Chairman, when necessary, and will bring in most of the contracts. I will also make ad hoc visits everywhere to see all are on their toes."

The Squadron Leader was in his natural element, giving orders for others to carry out.

There are times in the life of even the cleverest dodger when he knows he is beaten. At these times one must suppress the deep groan inwardly and outwardly produce that look of interest that convinces the martinet that you are willing.

I said, "It would seem that you have got everything worked out, Sir."

"I have indeed, Gooner." The Squadron Leader threw me his best salute.

I rose and returned a half-hearted salute.

Things have turned full circle. I am once again working for the Squadron Leader.

Also by Sir Arthur Lawrence

<u>Suicide In Mind</u>

Virginia Woolf : Cesare Pavese : Sarah Kane : Ernest Hemingway : Anne Sexton : Thomas Lovell Beddoes : Sylvia Plath : Hunter S Thompson.

Eight brilliant writers of international acclaim, with at least one thing in common – they all committed suicide.

Research in the UK and the USA has established that suicidal thoughts are more prevalent in writers than in any other profession. But what causes writers with suicide in mind to take the deadly step of committing the act?

That is the question which this book poses to the reader.

The eight essays contained in this book, which are in essence short biographies, will invite the reader to find common threads running through the lives of these writers and leading to their death by suicide. The usual suspects – drink, drugs and depression, will suggest themselves. They play their part, but they are only upon the surface. The reader will need to crawl below and into the psyche of these writers to discover why they have suicide in mind.

<u>Reviews</u>

George MacDonald Fraser: "Each biography has its own merits. I particularly liked Woolf and Hemingway."

M. Underhill: "Unusual book. Great subject." 5 stars

K. Sazdova: "Strongly recommended." 5 stars

Sirarthurlawrence@btinternet.com

Author Profile

Sir Arthur G. Lawrence has had an eclectic career - RAF officer, professional boxer, accountant, surveyor, investment fund manager, film producer/distributor, and theatrical angel. He has also been a senior executive in three of the largest PLCs in Europe. A keen advocate of the arts - particularly film and theatre - he is a former member of BAFTA, and currently a member of the Rose Theatre, Kingston and the British Film Institute. An all-round sportsman in his youth, Sir Arthur still plays golf and table-tennis. His published titles are *Suicide in Mind* and *Maralinga Man: Tales of the Squadron Leader*, and he lives in Kingston, Surrey.

Rowanvale Books

Publisher Information

Rowanvale Books provides publishing services to independent authors, writers and poets all over the globe. We deliver a personal, honest and efficient service that allows authors to see their work published, while remaining in control of the process and retaining their creativity. By making publishing services available to authors in a cost-effective and ethical way, we at Rowanvale Books hope to ensure that the local, national and international community benefits from a steady stream of good quality literature.

For more information about us, our authors or our publications, please get in touch.

www.rowanvalebooks.com
info@rowanvalebooks.com

Lightning Source UK Ltd.
Milton Keynes UK
UKHW01f1029110518
322461UK00002B/56/P

9 781911 240785